MATTHEW'S
Narrative
Portrait of
Disciples

MATTHEW'S
Narrative Portrait of Disciples

How the
Text-Connoted
Reader Is
Informed

Richard A. Edwards

TRINITY PRESS INTERNATIONAL
Harrisburg, Pennsylvania

Trinity Press International, P.O. Box 1321, Harrisburg, PA 17105
Trinity Press International is a division of the Morehouse Group

Library of Congress Cataloging-in-Publication Data

Edwards, Richard Alan.
    Matthew's narrative portrait of disciples : how the text-connoted reader is informed / Richard A. Edwards.
        p. cm.
    Includes bibliographical references and index.
    ISBN 1-56338-205-9 (pbk. : alk. paper)
    1. Bible. N.T. Matthew – Criticism, interpretation, etc.
I. Title.
BS2575.2.E375 1997
226.2'066–dc21   97-1708
                                                        CIP

Printed in the United States of America

97   98   99   00   01   10   9   8   7   6   5   4   3   2   1

CONTENTS

PREFACE

THIS BOOK is the application of a detailed definition of the narrative exegetical method. There are many different ways of defining and using a method which focuses on a story. Scholars have used a variety of different terms: literary-critical, story, reader response, etc. Most scholars combine it, in various ways, with redaction criticism. I find that such approaches are really different ways of using redaction criticism, that is, of seeking to find the theology of the editor and his/her *Sitz im Leben*.

I feel it is important to keep each method distinct. They are all limited but their individuality should be maintained to help understand the interpretation that is presented by each.

To demonstrate my understanding of the narrative method this study focuses on a specific feature of Matthew's narrative, a set of characters. It is an attempt to define and employ the method as distinct from others.

"Many thanks" to my graduate students who have raised interesting questions about this method as I tried to demonstrate its distinctiveness. And a special "thank you" to Michael Fuller for his detailed help in revising and editing this book. It is still my approach and style of exegesis but it is smoother and clearer because of Michael's help.

INTRODUCTION

THE GOSPEL OF MATTHEW is a narrative of the life of Jesus. It is not an essay, a letter, nor a theological treatise but a story which moves continuously from a beginning to its conclusion. Jesus is the primary character throughout the story. There are a few incidents in which he is not present or "on the scene." But even in these incidents the narrator makes it clear that the events relate directly to the presentation of Jesus. The response or reaction to the person of Jesus by a character (as an individual or group) is, however, not always positive and the narrator does not, at any point in the story, portray Jesus negatively. Although there is no other individual in the narrative as prominent as Jesus, the followers/disciples are clearly the second most significant character(s). Their portrayal, however, differs distinctly from the portrayal of Jesus. At times they are presented positively and at other times negatively. As a result, it is often not immediately clear how they are to be understood. Because the disciples are portrayed both positively and negatively, as a changing or inconsistent group of followers, their portrayal is complex. In addition, the word "disciple" is not always used consistently. Thus, an understanding of the disciples as characters in Matthew's narrative is not easy to grasp.

The exegetical method used to comprehend Matthew is important. Matthew has been assumed to be an editor, based on the *redaction*-critical approach, who revised and expanded the Gospel of Mark and thereby revealed his own theological concerns and interests. Because the editor has made significant changes to Mark's presentation of the disciples, some redaction critics have suggested an inconsistency in the gospel based primarily on the difference between traditions which the editor did not emend and those that were either emended or inserted. As a result, there are both positive and negative features of the disciples in Matthew's edited story. On the positive side, in 13:51, the disciples answer "yes" to Jesus' question, "Do you understand these things [parables]?"; and at Matt. 16:12 and 17:13 the narrator reports that they understood the meaning of Jesus' statement. Negatively, in 16:22–23 Peter is reported to rebuke Jesus for his statement about his death and resurrection, and Jesus addresses the disciples as those with "little faith" five times (6:30, 8:26, 14:31, 16:8, 17:20). Thus, the primary questions for a redaction critical approach are: What exactly is the

1

author's/editor's view of the disciples? What is his purpose in presenting an apparently inconsistent appraisal of the disciples?

In the past, in order to achieve a clear understanding of the disciples in Matthew, the disciple-related information from other gospels, and especially from the book of Acts, has been used as a primary source. Because Acts presents the disciples as significant respondents to Jesus' death and resurrection, any negative portrayal in Matthew's story has often been overlooked or considered insignificant. Given this information from outside Matthew, it is normal for many interpreters to produce a specific, positive understanding of Matthew's portrayal.[1]

A correct, historically accurate understanding of the disciples, however, has been a constant problem for the historical-critical scholar. The problem was increased when redaction critics began working within the Gospel of Mark. The redaction-critical method assumes that the *overall* theology of the author/editor is primary for determining the way various characters are presented in each gospel. Taken as a distinct theological work, the Gospel of Mark could be understood as a criticism of the disciples.[2] Since the disciples are presented in a favorable, if limited, way in the book of Acts and other portions of the New Testament, Mark's portrayal is most often considered unusual. Many have argued that the "redactor of Mark" presents the disciples as restricted followers of Jesus. Although it is possible to find reasons for assuming that Mark's criticism of the disciples is related to the condensed nature of his "story of Jesus,"[3] there has been little scholarly agreement about how such differing options can be judged. For example, Werner Kelber argues that Mark specifically portrayed the disciples as inadequate followers of Jesus. In contrast, Paul Achtemeier argues that the disciples' post-resurrection recognition of the true character of Jesus, which is not reported in Mark's story, was known by the people from whom Mark

---

1. The most important recent studies of the disciples in Matthew: Ulrich Luz, "The Disciples in the Gospel according to Matthew," in *The Interpretation of Matthew,* ed. G. Stanton (Philadelphia: Fortress, 1983), 98–128; Daniel Patte, "Prolegomena to a Study of the Disciples in Matthew," an unpublished paper presented at the SNTS Matthew Seminar, 1989; Andries G. van Aarde, "The Disciples in Matthew's Story," *Hervormde Teologiese* 5 (1994): 87–104; David B. Howell, "Jesus as the Model for Discipleship: Literary Criticism, Authorial Intention, and Redaction Criticism," chapter 6 in his Ph.D. dissertation, "Matthew's Inclusive Story," Oxford University, 1988; W. Carter, *Households and Discipleship: A Study of Matthew 19–20,* JSNTSup 1031 (Sheffield: Sheffield, 1994); Andrew H. Trotter, "Understanding and Stumbling: A Study of the Disciples' Understanding of Jesus and His Teaching in the Gospel of Matthew," Ph.D. diss., Cambridge University, 1993; Michael James Wilkens, "Named and Unnamed Disciples in Matthew: A Literary/Theological Study," in Lovering, ed., SBL Seminar Papers, 1991, 418–39.

2. Especially in Werner H. Kelber, *Mark's Story of Jesus* (Philadelphia: Fortress, 1979).

3. Paul J. Achtemeier, *Mark,* Proclamation Commentaries (Philadelphia: Fortress, 1986).

was writing and, therefore, that the disciples are portrayed as typical of those who did not comprehend Jesus' importance *until* the resurrection verified his significance. Thus, given the uniqueness of Mark when compared to the other synoptic gospels, it is clear that each evangelist has a distinct way of portraying the disciples.

Once the peculiarity of Mark's presentation of the disciples is suggested, comparing Mark with Matthew and Luke, who are assumed to use Mark's material, results in a recognition of the importance of these different editors and their theological emphases. Since Matthew and Luke are assumed to have been written later than Mark, they are usually understood to have a better and more detailed presentation of the disciples as the first followers of Jesus. The theology of the editor, Matthew, seems to place more emphasis on the disciples and Luke seems to move in the same direction.

Given such a redactional approach, it is clear that factors from both *within* and *outside* each gospel have been used to solve the problem of the editor's understanding of the disciples. However, since each gospel is a distinct narrative, is it adequate to combine such materials? Is it possible to find an approach that stays within the narrative of each gospel? Since the gospels are indeed narratives, the question has to be raised about an appropriate method for finding an answer to the apparent distinctiveness of each story.

It is the purpose of this study to define a narrative exegetical method and to use it to find a solution to the portrayal of the disciples in Matthew's story. However, there is at present a lack of agreement about the specifics of the narrative method. Some critics have used the term "literary" in a wide and inclusive way. It is often not clear what is meant by a literary analysis. There are also a variety of approaches to the gospels as "stories" — all of which are called a "narrative method." Because of such wide variation in the use of narrative criticism, it will take time before the specifics of the method are clarified and accepted by scholars. This study of Matthew is based on the need to focus on what I consider the distinctive methodological feature of the narrative approach — the implied reader.

Since the redaction-critical method focuses on the editor/author, there continues to be some confusion about the distinction between the way redaction critics and narrative critics understand the author of a gospel. Without a clear recognition of the difference between (1) the understanding of the editor/redactor and his/her audience in redaction criticism and (2) the implied author and implied reader in narrative criticism, the narrative-critical method is often considered simply a new aspect of the redactional approach and not a distinctly different method for exegesis.

Method

In order to define the narrative method used in this study, I begin by describing the redaction-critical approach and thereby help clarify how the narrative-critical method differs.

Redaction criticism, a development of form criticism, assumes that the author/editor emended or modified traditional, handed-down material in order to produce a document that would serve the purposes for which he was writing. There are two assumptions: first, the editor had a specific theological position which he was trying to communicate; second, the editor's understanding of the audience to which the gospel was directed was a major factor in determining both the wording and the construction of what was presented. As a result, redaction critics view the Gospel of Matthew as a theological statement in story form. Rather than writing an essay or statement of his beliefs and theology, the editor of Matthew constructed a story intended to convey his theological understanding of Jesus. Since the editor's theology, which lies behind the story, is assumed to be consistent, there should, obviously, be consistency within the story. For example, the editor's understanding of the disciples can be uncovered by combining and comparing all portions of the story in which the disciples are portrayed. Therefore in a redaction-critical analysis each incident can be removed from its place in the flow of the story, all similar ideas and themes located, and the results of the combined material used to uncover the overall purpose of the gospel. In addition, since the attitude of the audience which the editor addressed was as important as the editor's theology which guided him, some variation or difference may be present, but the overall result should be consistent. Redaction critics also argue that because the editor was working with traditions, he was partially committed to maintaining some of the features of the materials handed down. By studying the various changes, compositions, and traditions, the redaction critic can eventually reconstruct the editor's theology.

Narrative criticism differs from redaction criticism in a number of ways. Its primary assumption, because one is dealing with a narrative, rather than an essay, is that a narrative is a means of communication between the author and the reader. Since in studying the gospels the (1) historical or social context and (2) the real author or the historical audience are not known, it is best for the narrative critic to use the specifics of the story itself to seek a clear understanding of its purpose. The primary assumption of the narrative method, therefore, is that a distinction must be made between the real author, the implied author, and the narrator on one side of a communication model, and the real reader, the implied reader, and narratee on the other side.[4] The *narrator* is the individual who is literally telling the story to the *narratee*. In all the gospels, the narrator and narratee are never identified. The *real author* is the individual who wrote the story; the *real reader* is each individual, at *any* time or place, who reads the story or hears it being read. The *implied author* and the *implied reader* are hypothetical constructs based on the narrative itself. Rather than seeking to identify the real author, for whom we do not have historical information, the narrative critic seeks the implied author, basing his conclusion on the complete narrative. The focus of the narrative method, then, is upon the *implied reader,* a hypothetical construct based on the specific features of the story as it moves from beginning to the end.[5]

Given this understanding of a story, narrative criticism tries to answer the question, How has the hypothetical *implied reader* been informed, guided, or influenced by the story being told? Once the information given to the hypothetical *implied reader* has been carefully uncovered, it is possible to reach some limited conclusions about the intention of the implied author in a particular narrative. Thus, the emphasis in *redaction* criticism on the editor shifts in *narrative* criticism to the hypothetical implied reader.

Given this basic understanding of the narrative method, there is at this early stage in biblical scholars' application of the method, no agreed upon definition of how the implied reader should be uncovered. Definitions of the narrative method and its components differ and are at times imprecise. Many critics, who use what they call the "narrative method," focus on different issues. One of the major problems that accompanies a new method of biblical analysis, such as narrative criticism, is that it tends to be combined with other methods and is not given a

---

4. The primary books for beginning to understand narrative criticism are Seymour Chatman, *Story and Discourse: Narrative Structure in Fiction and Film* (Ithaca, N.Y.: Cornell University Press, 1978); idem., *Coming to Terms: The Rhetoric of Narrative in Fiction and Film* (Ithaca, N.Y.: Cornell University Press, 1990); Shlomith Rimmon-Kenan, *Narrative Fiction: Contemporary Poetics* (London and New York: Methuen, 1983); Wayne C. Booth, *The Rhetoric of Fiction* (Chicago and London: University of Chicago Press, 1961); Steven Mailloux, *Interpretative Conventions: The Reader in the Study of American Fiction* (Ithaca, N.Y., and London: Cornell University Press, 1982); idem., *Rhetorical Power* (Ithaca, N.Y. and London: Cornell University Press, 1989); Wolfgang Iser, *The Act of Reading: A Theory of Aesthetic Response* (Baltimore: Johns Hopkins University Press, 1974); Gerard Genette, *Narrative Discourse* (Ithaca, N.Y., and London: Cornell University Press, 1980); Meir Sternberg, *Expositional Modes and Temporal Ordering in Fiction* (Baltimore: Johns Hopkins University Press, 1978); idem., *The Poetics of Biblical Narrative: Ideological Literature and the Drama of Reading* (Bloomington: Indiana University Press, 1985). For the narrative study of Matthew see Jack Dean Kingsbury, *Matthew as Story* (Philadelphia: Fortress, 1986); David B. Howell, *Matthew's Inclusive Story: A Study in the Narrative Rhetoric of the First Gospel,* JSNT 42 (Sheffield: JSOT, 1990); Mark Alan Powell, *What Is Narrative Criticism?* Guides to Biblical Scholarship (Minneapolis: Fortress, 1990).

5. Cf. Powell, *What Is Narrative Criticism?*

full, independent test of its distinct possibilities and limits. In order to evaluate the narrative method, it should be carefully distinguished from historical, form, sociological, and — especially — redaction criticism.

Since narrative criticism as applied in this study is based on the assumption, unlike redaction criticism, that a narrative is a means of communication between author and reader, there is no initial concern for the historical background, that is, for identifying the author or for having access to sources. Rather than seeking the theological stance of the evangelist (the intention of the editor/redactor), the narrative critic tries to understand the *world of the narrative,* a unified entity which is the specific environment presented within the narrative. If our primary concern is to focus on what is presented to the implied reader and to discover how the implied reader is influenced, an important assumption is the concept of the *world of the narrative.* Each narrative creates an environment in which the story takes place. The world of the narrative is, by definition, blank at the beginning; it contains nothing, and as the story unfolds it is gradually presented or described, either indirectly or directly. As the story opens, the world of the narrative *begins* to be presented. In Mark, for example, the story begins with an introductory statement and a description of John the Baptist, who is then reported to baptize Jesus. In Matthew, the story begins with an introductory statement and a description of Jesus' genealogical background. In Luke, after a lengthy preliminary statement, the circumstances surrounding the birth of John the Baptist are presented in great detail. As each story progresses, more information becomes available and serves as the basis for the construction of that world. Thus, each narrative has its own way of initializing the world of that narrative and, as the story continues, new or modifying information is presented.

There is, as I indicated, a lack of clarity and agreement among biblical scholars about the narrative-critical method and the implied reader. For example, when literary critics analyze stories written and which take place in the twentieth century, the problem of historical and cultural location can be handled relatively easily. In a study of first-century narratives, however, such issues are difficult to handle. In addition, there are some biblical scholars, who consider themselves narrative critics, who refer to the "reader" but nevertheless continue to seek the "author's intention" as their primary analytical task. Although they use the terms narrative- or literary-critical approach, their analytical approach is redactional, not, as I understand it, narratival. To be a narrative approach the method should concentrate on the "implied reader" rather than the editor/author.

Therefore, the focus of this narrative analysis is to help clarify the *world of Matthew's narrative* by examining its influences on the implied reader. The question of the theology of the implied author must be put aside until the narrative-critical results are available.

One way to help understand the narrative method is to distinguish between (1) the world that is presented to the implied reader in the text, and (2) the assumptions which any *real* reader is likely to impose upon the text. By recognizing the importance of the cultural context of any real reader (of the first, third, tenth, or twentieth centuries), it might be easier to understand why some interpretations of Matthew's gospel are so different. The narrative method used in this study is limited, as with any method. Nevertheless, examining the *story* precisely and discovering how it influences the hypothetical implied reader will also help clarify where real readers, in specific cultural contexts, have overlooked, revised, or replaced certain elements of the story.

The term "gap" is a commonly used term in the narrative method to refer to the limited characteristics of any narrative world. Because not everything about the narrative world is presented to the implied reader — that is, because there are *gaps* in the story — each *real* reader can fill gaps in different ways. For example, the word "rabbi" is not defined in Matthew's story but used negatively. Some real readers, however, assume a rabbi is a highly respected religious leader and thereby have a positive understanding of the term. Identifying the negative use of the term would not necessarily guarantee a "correct" interpretation but, rather, would help clarify those features of the text that encourage a reader (*real reader*) to insert his assumptions and biases. By seeking to understand how the implied reader is informed, one begins to uncover the specifics of the narrative world.

The advantage of the narrative method I propose is that it accepts the limits of the text and recognizes the search for the rationale that lies behind the various interpretations that have, and continue to be, proposed. Can the reasons for varied interpretations be easily understood? Once the narrative method has been pushed to its legitimate limits, its advantages and disadvantages will be clearer. It will then be easier to use this approach with other methods to seek a more complete understanding of the Gospel of Matthew. This study uses the narrative method as an initial stage in the exegetical process. A critical, careful combination of methods will be required once this method is clearly defined and applied.

Real Reader and Text-Connoted Reader (Implied Reader)

As noted above, this narrative method focuses on the implied reader as someone addressed by the implied author. It is generally agreed that the *real author,* a specific, historical individual, can have, and often does

have, different values and points of view from those in the narrative.[6]
Likewise, *real readers* from the first, third, or twentieth century would
respond differently based on their backgrounds and cultural contexts.
Because the distinction between the implied and real reader has not been
clearly recognized or acknowledged, the narrative method used in this
study of Matthew will emphasize the implied reader.

The implied reader is a hypothetical construct built from the details
of the text.[7] However, the word "implied" could suggest that it refers to
the intention of the real author, as is common in redaction criticism. The
method used in this study is based primarily on the importance of the
hypothetical nature of the implied reader. It does not refer to the *original audience,* a focus that is common within redaction criticism. Rather,
"implied reader" is a technical term, following Seymour Chatman and
others, used to describe a non-real reader whose information and attitudes are determined only *by the narrative world* of the story under
analysis. The narrative, by definition, is a context or world limited because of its size. The narrative critic is required to work within the limits
of the world of each narrative. If a *real* reader interprets the meaning of
words or phrases based on information about the cultural context of
the author rather than the specifics presented in the story itself, he is
imposing material upon the narrative not specifically stated within the
narrative, in other words, that is not part of the narrative's world. This
method assumes that the implied reader has a basic acquaintance with
the language used, but that any particular word or phrase can be given
specific meaning within the story as it unfolds.

Because of the varied meanings that critics have attached to the
word "implied," the term "implied reader" has been used differently.
Many scholars who identify themselves as narrative critics use "implied
reader" to refer to a theoretical, first-century reader — someone that the
real author or editor had in mind as the recipient of this story. For these
critics, the term "implied" is assumed to refer to something in the mind
of the editor. Such an understanding is therefore simply a variation of
the redaction-critical method and the search for the editor/redactor's theology; it is an attempt to be more specific about the *Sitz im Leben* of
the editor as a way of clarifying his theology. Such critics use the term
"implied" as one way of describing the theology of the author/editor
because the term is based on the author/editor's understanding of the
audience addressed by the story. As a result, it is redaction analysis and
not narrative criticism.

---

6. Howell, *Inclusive Story,* esp. 161–204; Chatman, *Coming to Terms.*
7. Rimmon-Kenan, *Narrative Fiction,* 59–70; Thomas M. Leitch, *What Stories Are:
Narrative Theory and Interpretation* (University Park and London: Pennsylvania State
University Press, 1986), 148–65.

To help clarify my use of the term "implied reader," I suggest that a more descriptive term for this aspect of the narrative method is *text-connoted reader*. The word "connote" is usually defined with the word "imply"; it is something not explicitly stated (denoted) but rather is something intended by the words or events of the narrative. The combination "text-connoted," therefore, refers to the implications involved in the specifics of the story itself, the *world* of that narrative. The information presented to the text-connoted reader can be uncovered only by analyzing the details of the narrative and the world of that narrative. The text-connoted reader is a hypothetical construct based upon the world of the narrative, distinct from the redactional *Sitz im Leben*. The redactional approach can refer to a "reader," based on a possible construction of the cultural or historical environment of a real reader in the first century, and therefore poses a distinction from the non-real, hypothetical text-connoted reader of this narrative method.

The term "text-connoted reader" must also not be confused with a "first reader," a term that a number of us have used as a primary part of the narrative approach. The "first reader" concept is based on an assumption that one could historically reconstruct a person of the first century who had not previously been exposed to this story when it was "first" heard or read. In other words, the "first reader" is assumed to be a historical individual and therefore a *possible historical real reader* and is not the focus of the narrative method.

The text-connoted reader (hereafter written as T-CR), constructed from the data in the text, is a useful hypothetical construction. Once carefully delineated by a careful examination of the world of the narrative, the concept will greatly assist in clarifying the specifics and gaps of Matthew's narrative.

A narrative does not, of course, present every detail about any character, action, or situation. As a result, an important factor in informing the T-CR is not only the details of the story but also the material missing from the narrative world, the so-called "gaps." It is important to recognize that a "view of the text as a system"[8] can help in finding whether the T-CR does or does not have the information required to fill the gaps. That is, all of the story which precedes a specific incident supplies the information which might enable the T-CR to fill the gap. The narrative critic must work with the flow of the narrative to construct a unified system based on the information presented in the narrative and the order in which it is arranged. Since no story can supply all the information which any reader would need to achieve a complete, elaborate understanding of the world of the narrative, there are "gaps" in every narrative.

A "gap," therefore, is an opening or missing element in the narrative

---

8. Rimmon-Kenan, *Narrative Fiction,* 119.

which for the T-CR might be filled in with other elements already presented in the narrative world. For example, the mention of a name, such as Abraham (Matt. 1:1), which has obviously not been used previously, is initially a "gap" for the T-CR. There may be other incidents later in the story in which the name is used and, as a result, the name will have more context. A real reader, in contrast, can fill gaps with non-story data from his own world, often historical and cultural information.[9] The T-CR is informed *only* by the specifics of the narrative world under analysis from the beginning of the narrative, and *not* from sources beyond it, nor from events/descriptions which take place later in the story. For example, the portrait of the disciples must be founded on the way they are presented as the story progresses and not based on non-story material. There can be, by definition, only one T-CR. In contrast, there are obviously innumerable and very different real readers. The only way the T-CR can fill in gaps at a specific point in the flow of the story is by relating the details of the current incident with the information *already given* to the T-CR in the previous events in the narrative world.

How, then, since we are by definition real readers, can such a method be put into practice? By working within the text, following the order in which it is presented, and noting those portions of the narrative which are given some meaning in a direct way, we can locate the data available in the world of the narrative. It is a mistake for a narrative critic to assume that the original audience can be reconstructed and its attitude about the author's intention uncovered. For example, some critics have argued that the "implied readers" (note the plural) could be assumed to understand when the author of Matthew quotes from a specific text, could recognize the quotation, and could use their understanding of the wider context to reach a deeper insight about the message being presented.[10] Given the definition of T-CR stated above, the use of the term "implied readers" (plural) indicates that scholars have interpreted the implied reader/T-CR as a hypothetical, original audience of real readers, an approach similar to the uses of *Sitz im Leben* in redaction criticism. The narrative method to be used in this study of Matthew argues that before such historical information can be brought into the interpretation of the narrative, the narrative world must be carefully defined.

By analyzing the way the T-CR is being informed and influenced by the narrative, the details of the world of the narrative itself will be clearly delineated. Given the recognized variation in the way the disci-

---

9. This is an issue that is often overlooked or considered irrelevant. See Powell, *Narrative Criticism*, 72, 97.

10. Andrew T. Lincoln, "Matthew — A Story for Teachers?" in *The Bible in Three Dimensions: Essays in Celebration of Forty Years of Biblical Studies in the University of Sheffield*, ed. David J. A. Clines, Stephen E. Fowl, and Stanley E. Porter (Sheffield: JSOT Press, 1990), 109.

ples are presented in the New Testament, the problem of the disciples as characters has been a difficult problem for many years. Since the narrative method is limited to the narrative world of each specific story, the primary question for this study is: "How is the T-CR influenced to comprehend or understand the disciples in Matthew?"

Characters

Within narrative criticism, characters are defined as individuals or groups presented/portrayed in the world of the narrative. "Characterization" is a term to describe the techniques used in the narrative which guide the T-CR to attach specific traits or attributes to the characters. For example, John the Baptist is first presented in Matthew's story when the narrator reports that he preaches, that he was referred to by Isaiah, that he wears certain clothes, eats certain food, and that he baptized many people. As the story continues, these factors can be used as a context in which to comprehend later reports of his actions or words.

Therefore one crucial aspect of a narrative analysis is the need to recognize those features of the narrative world that will supply the basis for the T-CR's understanding of the individuals presented in the story. Although many critics describe characterization as an accumulation of traits[11] which can be applied to any person within the narrative, some have argued that this approach is too simple.[12] Various traits can be applied to a specific character based on direct information from the narrator ("telling") or based on the implications of words or actions ("showing"). If these traits are inconsistent or contradictory, the T-CR is given a variance and does not, at that moment in the flow of the story, have a way of reaching a sensible conclusion. When an obvious solution is not available, the T-CR may receive more information further along in the narrative which might help solve the dilemma.

To understand the disciples as characters in Matthew, it is necessary to analyze the way in which they are presented to the T-CR — the way they are characterized. Since the disciples are present in many places throughout the story, it is inadequate merely to combine all specific references about their abilities or limits. Such a procedure might be appropriate within redaction criticism, assuming that the author/editor has a consistent point of view throughout the story. Within narrative criticism, however, any character who appears more than once is presented to the T-CR in different contexts and, obviously, at different moments in the development of the story. Therefore, it is important to examine

---

11. Rimmon-Kenan, *Narrative Fiction*, 36–40.
12. Leitch, *Stories*, 148–65.

not only the details of any appearance, but, in addition, to study that particular event in relation to the previous appearances, those incidents where the character is portrayed in some other context.[13]

The T-CR is influenced to understand and recognize traits of a character (or group of individuals) by five different features of a narrative. "The Calming of the Storm" (Matt. 8:23–27) will be used as an example.

> [23]And when he got into the boat, his disciples followed him. [24]And behold there arose a great storm on the sea, so that the boat was being swamped by the waves; but he was asleep. [25]And they went and woke him, saying, "Save, Lord; we are perishing." [26]And he said to them, "Why are you afraid, O men of little faith?" Then he rose and rebuked the winds and the sea; and there was a great calm. [27]And the men marveled, saying, "What sort of man is this that even the winds and sea obey him?"

- **Action.** The narrator reports that the character performs a particular deed. "And they *went* and *woke* him..." (8:25). If this is the only information the T-CR has, it is not very clear about the rationale for such action.

- **Words spoken.** The narrator reports or quotes a character's words. "And they went and woke him, saying, '*Save, Lord; we are perishing*'" (8:25). As with action, spoken words are limited in conveying information about the character(s) involved.

- **Description.** The narrator reports specific details about the character. "And the men *marveled,* saying..." (8:27). The narrator reports that they marvel, i.e., the T-CR is given information about their internal response to an event. This is more revealing. The disciples are impressed and the quotation helps to evaluate this reaction. The majority of these instances are more precise in suggesting traits to the T-CR, especially if the narrator is considered reliable.

- **Reaction of *other* characters in the story.** The narrator reports how one character or group responds with actions or words; in this instance, how Jesus reacts to the disciples' action and words. "And he *said to them, 'Why are you afraid, O men of little faith?'*" (8:26). In addition to the specific details of Jesus' reaction, the T-CR's previous information about Jesus, who responds, must be considered. The respondent's (Jesus') own attitude could also be described by the narrator. The comprehension of this particular reaction depends upon many other related values and judgments that are part of the narrative world presented up to this point in the story.

---

13. Cf. ibid., 148–65.

- **The expectation expressed by *other* characters in the story.** The sequence or flow of the narrative presents what other individuals in the story expect from a character. In 8:26 this is involved when Jesus questions the disciples about their fear and calls them "men of little faith." Jesus' teaching in chapters 5–7, which precedes this event, presents not only Jesus' understanding of his task but his understanding of those individuals who abide by the law and prophets. The speech thereby gives the T-CR a context in which to place the criticism stated in 8:26.

To understand the characterization of a group like the disciples, one is required to analyze both (1) the *specific incident* in which they act, speak, respond, etc., and (2) the *context* of the incident, which helps the T-CR attach meaning to the words used.

The T-CR can be informed in a variety of ways to attach traits to individuals or groups within the story. Not only is a specific event itself important, but all of the material from the world of the narrative, that is, the context in which events occur, helps the T-CR comprehend what is presented. Matthew's story is primarily a sequence of short incidents. The story is told in small action/speech units which contain little explanation from the narrator about the circumstances surrounding the incident or about the thoughts of the characters. This differs from modern stories, in which the narrator spends more time describing the people involved, the environment in which the story occurs, and often uses a significant amount of time informing the T-CR about the attitudes and/or thoughts in the mind of one or more of the characters, sometimes called "inside information." Because the narrative of Matthew does not contain many such descriptions, the T-CR of this narrative world does not receive much "inside" information about a character's actions or words. It is necessary, therefore, to place the specifics of an incident in the context of the world presented by the narrative itself in order to understand how the T-CR is informed.

Since most of the T-CR's information comes from the actions and words of the characters themselves, the most important and informative data for a study of the characterization of the disciples are the *interactions* (in word or deed) with other characters, including words addressed to the disciples and their responses/reactions to such words or situations. In these interactions or responses, there is usually more specific information given by the context, and therefore the context is crucial in finding how the T-CR can comprehend a response. For example, if an action is reported by the narrator with *no* mention of the circumstances and/or the reasons that caused the individual to act as reported, the only basis for understanding the deed would be the previous information about the person who did the action and/or the response of those who witness it. If one character or set of characters, such as the disciples, are reported to respond in different situations as the story unfolds, the previous information presented is necessary to this method in uncovering the T-CR. For example, when Jesus' action brings forth a question from the disciples, the T-CR has been given the immediate context and, because so much is known about Jesus himself from prior narrative, the T-CR has a significant amount of information from which to gain a fuller understanding of the reason for the question and thereby to attach a trait or attribute to the disciples.

Thus, to understand what the narrator is saying about the disciples in Matthew, it is necessary to examine those incidents where the disciples are portrayed and the context in which they took place. The primary questions are: How is the T-CR being informed by the narrator about the disciples? What techniques are being used and what evaluations are being presented?

Character-Shaping Incidents

What specifically in Matthew's story influences the T-CR in understanding the disciples?

To understand the impact of the narrative on the T-CR, the five features that affect characterization must be carefully recorded and their immediate contextual implications noted. Each incident in Matthew's story in which the disciples are "on scene" has to be analyzed to locate any of the five elements that can guide the T-CR. There are many incidents that record no interaction, or very limited interaction. If the disciples, for example, are reported to have heard Jesus speak certain words, it is obviously an important event for the disciples. If, however, there is no indication, at that time or place, of their response, it is not a character-shaping incident but a situation that possibly helps set the context for a later event. Therefore, the context, the material that *precedes* the character-shaping incident, is important in establishing the background for the T-CR's understanding of the narrator's presentation of the disciples.

In a narrative in which Jesus is clearly the main character and the focus of attention, the characteristics of all others in the story are heavily influenced by the way they interact with Jesus. Therefore the starting point for this study of the disciples in Matthew must be a recognition of the centrality of Jesus within the narrative. There is no portion of the gospel that does not focus on Jesus, though there are incidents in which Jesus cannot be listed as the *principal* character. However, in such instances, Jesus is still the focus of the event. In Matthew, Jesus is an authoritative figure. His reliability and status are reemphasized in many ways; he functions both as a guide and standard from which the T-CR can judge others. His statements about the disciples are primary, his commands are assumed to be authoritative, and his criticisms, which are more justified because of the way he is portrayed, are crucial in influencing the T-CR. The disciples in Matthew appear more often than any other person or group except for Jesus and, therefore, the T-CR has more opportunity to be informed both by the narrator's statements about them and by their own actions or responses. Since the disciples are presented in different ways at various points in the narrative, i.e., as changeable or developing characters, the T-CR must coordinate, in sequence, the specific implications of each significant or character-shaping incident.

Once the disciples' character-shaping incidents have been defined, all the material between the character-shaping incidents must be carefully reviewed in order to recognize its impact on the T-CR's comprehension of the specific features of the character-shaping incident. For example, Jesus' speeches are especially crucial for detailing his *expectations* of the disciples; if the incident focuses on Jesus' reactions to the disciples' words and/or deeds, the context is important for the T-CR in grasping why Jesus acts or speaks as he does.

A character-shaping incident, therefore, is an event in which the T-CR is given enough information, most often by means of a *response*, to be able to attach one or more attributes to the disciples. There are, of course, many incidents in Matthew in which the disciples are active. Because narrative analysis emphasizes the T-CR, however, the character-shaping incidents are primarily those incidents from which the T-CR receives enough information *either* to add a new, distinct trait to the disciples *or* to modify one or more of the currently applicable traits.

Within Matthew's story the disciple character-shaping incidents are fundamentally those that contain a definite response by a disciple or the disciple group to an action or saying. For example, when the narrator reports that a person acts in a certain way, or says a certain thing, the report itself supplies a limited but significant amount of information about that character. The T-CR in such an instance is given information which, in combination with background material from the narrative world presented up to that point, would help fill in the gaps. When, however, the narrative presents details that seek to explain the situation that *called forth* the response, the response (action and/or statement) can be understood more clearly. Because the narrator of Matthew's gospel gives the T-CR little *direct* information about the disciples, the T-CR is required to hypothesize, make judgments, or fill in the gaps, based on the narrative world of this story. As a result, when the principal character, Jesus, directs any words or action toward the disciples, their response to that situation reveals more about them than any other statement, and is thereby a character-shaping incident. When the incident is viewed within the specific *context* of the action or statement, it is much easier to recog-

nize how the T-CR has also been informed by the narrative world about
the disciples' response.

Given this definition of the T-CR and the narrative world, I suggest
that there are eleven disciple character-shaping incidents in the Gospel
of Matthew.

1. The Call of Peter, Andrew, James, and John (4:18–22).

2. The Stilling of the Storm (8:18–27).

3. The Disciples' Affirmative Response to the Parables (13:51–52).

4. The Walking on the Water (14:22–33).

5. The Caesarea Philippi Interaction (16:5–23).

6. The Disciples' Experience of the Transfiguration of Jesus
   (17:1–13).

7. The Dialogue about Riches (19:23–20:28).

8. Judas Iscariot Becomes the Betrayer (26:14–25).

9. Peter's Denial (26:30–58 [59–68] 69–75).

10. Judas Iscariot Repents and Commits Suicide (27:3–10).

11. The Disciples Meet the Risen Lord (28:16–20).

In this study, each incident will be examined in detail to explain how
the T-CR is informed. Once these specifics have been noted, the context — the material leading up to the incident under consideration —
must be examined to find any content that would guide the T-CR to respond. For example, the study of incident two (8:18–27), "The Stilling
of the Storm," begins with an analysis of the way the T-CR is guided by
the details in 8:18–27 and then surveys 4:23–8:16, the context following incident one (4:18–22), to find the way the flow of the story helps
set the stage for incident two.

Graphics

An important part of a narrative analysis is the capability of viewing the
narrative as a complete, connected, flowing entity. In order to communicate to MY reader (you) some of the interrelated data that a narrative
approach must consider, the gospel must be viewed as a whole, as a
complete unit, that is, as a narrative world. It is important to see certain

Disciple Response Analysis
Matthew

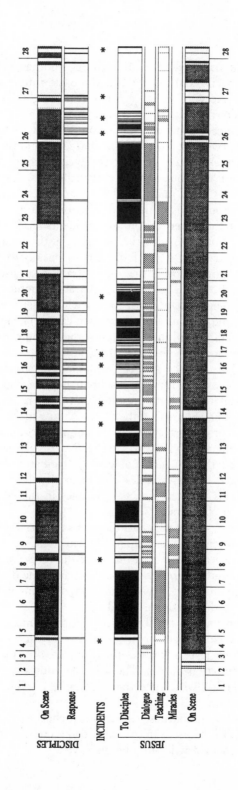

features of the narrative in relation to one another. Lists of citations or tables with specific data are useful for basic information but are not adequate for showing where certain items might be clustered, or, in contrast, where they do *not* occur.

The charts accompanying each chapter display the relationship in the story world between Jesus, the main character, and the disciples, important secondary characters. Since it is the connection between them and their interaction with one another that is the most important part of the story for the T-CR to understand the disciples, the chart displays the information about Jesus in the lower section and the information about the disciples in the upper section. The incidents section between the *Jesus* and *Disciples* portions, with the asterisks, is the focus because we can see (1) how often and when Jesus acts or speaks to the disciples; and (2) when the story informs the T-CR of any response by the disciples. The asterisks show where the eleven character-shaping incidents occur.

The twenty-eight chapters of Matthew's gospel are listed, in relative length, along the top and bottom of each chart. The lower five-row portion diagrams information about Jesus: the medium-shaded areas in the *On Scene* row mark the portion of the story where Jesus is present; the light-shaded areas in the *Miracles* row mark where specific healings or nature miracles are the focus; the light-shaded areas in the *Teaching* row mark where sayings of Jesus are quoted and where there is no conversation; the light-shaded areas in the *Dialogue* row mark incidents in which Jesus' sayings or deeds respond to questions or comments from another character; the dark-shaded areas in the *To Disciples* row mark moments when it is clear that an action or saying (from any of the four units below) is directed at the disciples. For example, the narrator specifically states that Jesus was teaching the disciples in the verse just before the long speech in chapters 5–7.

The top portion of each chart diagrams two basic features of the portrait of the disciples: the medium-shaded areas in the *On Scene* row mark where the narrator states that the disciples are present; the dark-shaded areas in the *Response* row show where the disciples act or speak in response to an action, saying, question, or command from some other character(s) in the narrative world.

Thus when lines in the lower *Jesus* portion and the upper *Disciples* portion come close together in the middle of each chart, the chart depicts how often Jesus addresses the disciples, directly or indirectly, and when an interaction occurs. The asterisks indicate those points in the narrative where I will argue that a definite disciple character-shaping incident has occurred.

In the following analysis, an expanded chart of each incident and its context will also be used. In the expanded section, a few more details of the narrative world will often be displayed.

Character-Shaping Incident One:

THE CALL OF PETER, ANDREW, JAMES, AND JOHN
Matt. 4:18–22

THIS FIRST disciple character-shaping incident (4:18–22) gives the T-CR initial information about people as "followers" of Jesus. As displayed in the chart, this is the first time in the story that any followers of Jesus are "on scene." Everything previous to this point in the story is considered the framework which has focused on the main character, Jesus, and on one individual, John the Baptist, who recognizes Jesus as the one he is expecting, the one who ranks above him. Now that the T-CR has been given explicit information about Jesus, the narrator has Jesus "on scene" for almost all of the remainder of the story. At this time, the beginning of Jesus' ministry, some "followers" are portrayed for the first time.

The expanded chart of incident one shows that this is the first time Jesus speaks or acts toward any follower, and it is the followers' first response to any action, teaching, or question. They have not been part of the story before this incident (i.e., not "on scene"). The four men who decide to follow Jesus are not given any specific title or descriptive identity other than that they will be made "fishers of people." At this point in the world of this narrative, the word "disciple" has not yet been used.

What are the details in 4:18–22 that help the T-CR understand the followers?

Details of Event

The narrator reports the response of two pairs of brothers to Jesus' request that they follow him.

> [18]As he walked by the Sea of Galilee, he saw two brothers, Simon who is called Peter and Andrew his brother, casting a net into the sea; for they were fishermen. [19]And he said to them, "Come after

19

me, and I will make you fishers of people." [20]Immediately they left
their nets and followed him. [21]And going on from there he saw two
other brothers, James the son of Zebedee and John his brother,
in the boat with Zebedee their father, mending their nets, and he
called them. [22]Immediately they left the boat and their father, and
followed him.

Prior to the response of these four men, the narrator describes the
situation in which the response occurs: they are at work, carrying out
the requirements of their occupation as fishermen. The incident focuses
on Jesus' statement, both a command and promise directed to two pairs
of brothers, and on their reaction: each pair immediately leaves the oc-
cupational activity and follows Jesus. Jesus' statement is the equivalent
of an imperative ("come after me") followed by a reference to the future, a promise: "I will make you fishers of people" (4:19). Thus, as a
source for understanding the four individuals as characters, the narrator
reports an action which is a response to words of Jesus.

No other information is given which might explain the reason for
their action, such as a narrator's omniscient statement about their
thoughts or attitudes. In the "call" of the second pair of brothers, the
narrator does not quote Jesus but merely states that Jesus "called them"
(4:21). Their response, however, is described in the same way; that is,
the narrator reports, "they left the boat and their father, and followed
him" (4:22).

Matt. 4:18–22 qualifies as a character-shaping incident because it
contains a specific, defined response and also because it is the first time
that Jesus asks anyone to follow him. As a result, it depicts *both* the
response of the four men to his command *and* an indication of Jesus'
understanding of his purpose and goals.

The call of the four fishermen, which is the introduction of the disciples, is compact and limited. There are no explanations from the
narrator about the fishermen's thoughts or their rationale for reacting
as they do in this first portrayal. Therefore the T-CR is confronted with
a gap and may receive more information to have a more specific portrait
of these followers. Because of its repetition by the narrator in describing their action, emphasis is placed upon the word "follow" (4:20, 22).
Jesus uses metaphorical language — that they will be made "fishers of
people" — to indicate why they should follow him. The incident, therefore, portrays these four fishermen as individuals who are interested in
Jesus' command promise and act upon it.

Although the narrator does not explain the reasons for their response, Jesus gives a reason for asking them to follow him: "I will
make you fishers of people." The T-CR is thereby guided to see that the
fishermen find this goal highly attractive — enough to drop everything at

Disciple Character-Shaping Analysis #1: Matthew 4:18–22
Expanded Section: Matthew 1:1–5:3

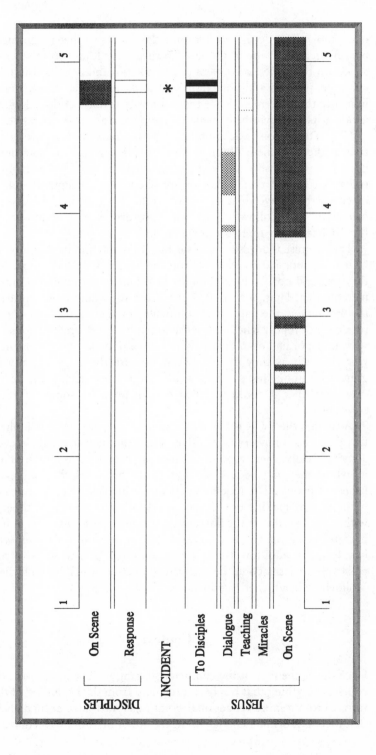

once and follow Jesus. As a result, the T-CR has been informed of a possible feature to be found later in the story: Jesus' promise has great appeal to these men who seem to like the possibility of becoming "fishers of people." In addition, Jesus' authority is another factor that could influence the fishermen. Since that authority is not mentioned within the incident itself, it will be considered below as part of the context.

Characterization is accomplished by the narrator's report of the action of the four men: "Immediately they [Peter and Andrew] left their nets [James and John: the boat and their father] and followed him." The traits that best fit their behavior are obedience, perceptivity, and quick reaction; they leave their means of livelihood with no hesitation ("immediately") to "follow" Jesus. Since no further explanation is offered, the T-CR receives limited information.

The promise that Jesus makes is metaphorical and builds upon the information supplied by the narrator: the brothers are fishermen. As such they respond positively to the idea of fishing for people. The impact of metaphorical language upon a character, especially one appearing for the first time in the narrative, is difficult to judge on its own. The narrator does not report whether the fishermen have had any previous contact with Jesus, or had even heard about him, and makes no statement about why they act as they do. However, because the T-CR already knows quite a bit about Jesus at this point in the story, such a gap leaves the possibility that it could be filled or explained by some future action or event.

Although the T-CR is left with an incomplete picture, the limited portrayal of the followers is positive. The fishermen leave their everyday activity because they respond to this man, presented as a man of authority whom they may believe can do what he promises, that is, make them fishers of people. The indefiniteness of the incident requires the T-CR to fill in gaps by making use of previous details, the context of the incident within the world that the narrative has established up to this point. The narrator has given the T-CR a favorable impression of the four who follow Jesus. In addition, the narrative indicates that those who respond positively to Jesus could be referred to as "followers," giving the word "follow" a heightened significance.

Context

Since this is the first of the character-shaping incidents, its context is, of course, everything that has been presented from the beginning of the narrative. From a more redactional point of view, I have argued elsewhere that there is a distinct change in the nature of the story immediately after this incident and that the call of the four fishermen is the conclusion of the introduction (1:1–4:22). [1] However, the *framework* of a narrative is normally defined as that portion at the beginning which establishes basic characteristics and features of the narrative world; it supplies foundational information for the T-CR. Matthew begins his story not with the *career* of Jesus but with a variety of incidents about his family, birth, relation to the Father, etc., which inform the T-CR of basic principles and concepts which will be functional and foundational throughout the world of this narrative. In addition to Jesus' genealogy and the circumstances of his birth, other incidents in the framework section are Jesus' relation to John the Baptist, his baptism, his identification as the Son of the Father, and his resistance to Satan's temptation.

Features of the framework important for understanding this disciple character-shaping event and the world of the narrative are:

1. The "Father" is active within the environment that Jesus has now entered. This is evident in the way the genealogy is structured (1:17); the way the Magi are guided by the star (2:1–12); the way the Magi and Joseph are guided by the Father's messengers in dreams (1:20–21; 2:12; 2:19, 22); the way the narrator shows the direct relation between present events and the Father's word from the past — the "fulfillment quotations" (1:22–23; 2:15, 17–18; 3:3; 4:14–16); the way the Father speaks at the baptism (3:17), which affirms John's recognition of his status (3:14); and the way Jesus is led by the Spirit into the wilderness where he resists temptation by his own reference to written traditions (4:1–11). The narrator shows that Jesus, the son of the Father, is an individual with divine status; he is part of the Father's plan and in direct contact with the Father. Thus the T-CR has been given the kind of information that makes it easier to understand why the fishermen might respond as drastically as they do.

Jesus is the Messiah and Son of the Father. In addition to the narrator's direct statements, this is obvious for the T-CR at the baptism when the voice from heaven speaks not to Jesus but to those who witness the event (3:17). It is also evident in the temptation when two of Satan's commands for specific action from Jesus begin with the phrase: "If you are the son of God..." (4:3, 6). Jesus himself refers to the written tradition and is thus aligned with the narrator's reliability (4:4, 7, 10). For the T-CR, Jesus is portrayed in a consistent and continuous manner.

2. The narrator reports some inside information, that is, he sometimes presents to the T-CR the thoughts or attitudes which are in the minds of certain characters. This informs the T-CR that the state-

---

1. Richard A. Edwards, *Matthew's Story of Jesus* (Philadelphia: Fortress Press, 1985), 11–18.

ment belongs to the narrator and that it might be important later as the story develops. For example, the content of Joseph's dreams is presented directly by the narrator (1:20–21; 2:13, 19–20), who also demonstrates, in the fulfillment quotations, his understanding of the relation between present events and the promises of the Father recorded in the past (1:22–23; 2:15, 17–18; 3:3; 4:14–16). The positive connection of these framework incidents/items with the *past* is heavily stressed in the genealogy, in the fulfillment quotations, and in the temptation.

3. "Righteousness" or "justness" is stated directly by the narrator as an attribute of Joseph (1:19) and illustrated in his actions. He is an individual who not only listens to the messages that come from the Father, but also recognizes their importance and obeys them (1:24–25; 2:14–15, 21). Thus the T-CR has been shown a character who is an open recipient to the Father's message and thus a personification of a God-respecting person.

4. The T-CR can expect a negative reaction to Jesus from the Jewish authorities. Herod is portrayed as an individual who promises support (2:7–8), but then acts violently when he does not get his own way (2:16). As the story progresses, response to Jesus, despite his character and status, could be negative from people with power.

5. Jesus' authority as Christ/Messiah is clearly presented. John the Baptist, described as someone dependent upon the Father and the tradition God represents (3:1–6), recognizes Jesus' status and accepts his words (3:14–15). Thus the T-CR has been shown another individual who is clearly in close contact with the Father. In response to John the Baptist's question about whether he should baptize Jesus, Jesus' first quoted statement, "Let it be so now; for it is proper for us in this way to fulfill all righteousness" (3:15), convinces John the Baptist that he should consent to the request and that it is based on their acceptance of the Father's authority.

6. There are a number of instances of metaphoric material in the teaching of John the Baptist: the brood of vipers (3:7), the bearing of fruit that befits repentance (3:8), an ax at the root of the trees (3:10), and the winnowing fork (3:12). Thus, someone in close contact with the Father uses this kind of language to express his message. When Jesus describes the followers as "fishers of people," the T-CR already has been informed of the appropriateness and importance of such metaphoric language. Jesus' message about the impact of the future is presented in a form that requires anticipation on the part of the T-CR.

With the framework as the basic context of this first incident, the T-CR is informed of many items which help establish the world of this narrative and could be important in understanding the portrayal of the disciples.

Immediate Context

The immediate context, that is, the verses or incident (4:12–17) preceding the call of the four fishermen, contains the narrator's report that Jesus withdrew after his temptation by Satan (4:1–11) to the area around the Sea of Galilee. The reason, says the narrator, was the arrest of John the Baptist. This connection with John is emphasized even further in the next verses in the fulfillment quotation which cites Isaiah's words about a great light seen by those who live in Galilee. This is another metaphoric expression similar to those used by John the Baptist. As a climax to this report from the narrator, Jesus' preaching is reported in words *identical* to the basic message of John the Baptist: "Repent, for the kingdom of heaven is at hand" (3:2; 4:17). In this way, the T-CR is influenced both to compare John the Baptist and Jesus and to recognize their close but differing relationships to the Father, since it is clear that Jesus has a status above John.

After being baptized and tempted, Jesus is depicted as the Son of God who speaks (4:17) on behalf of the Father. His message is part of the Father's plan; the Father has been, and still is, directly involved in this world. The term "kingdom of heaven," mentioned earlier (3:2) by John the Baptist, is used at the beginning of each man's career in this narrative world. The call to "repent, for the kingdom of heaven is at hand" functions, therefore, as a thesis statement. The T-CR is informed that John's preaching (3:7–12), reported in some detail immediately after John's statement about the kingdom, is a specific way of comprehending the thesis about the kingdom. John the Baptist's emphasis is on the future ("Who warned you to flee from the wrath to come?" 3:7) and its impact on the people of God ("children to Abraham," 3:9).

With this information having been presented to the T-CR, what does Jesus mean, then, when he repeats the same message? ("Repent, for the kingdom of heaven is at hand.") The message begins with an imperative ("repent") and is followed by an explanation ("for the kingdom of heaven is at hand") introduced by *gar*.[2] Because the narrator neither reports any response to the statement nor indicates a definite context, it gives the T-CR a broad and indefinite meaning. Such an imperative requires a specific reaction which should be based on what is anticipated in the immediate future. Only because of the authority and position that Jesus holds would anyone pay attention to such a requirement. Because it is immediately followed by the call of the four fishermen, the T-CR is informed of Jesus' meaning by the direct connection between the thesis statement and the incident, and by the fact that Jesus' mission is un-

---

2. Richard A. Edwards, "Narrative Implications of γαρ in Matthew," *CBQ* 52 (1990): 636–55.

like John the Baptist's in that he seeks followers. Since Jesus' preaching at this point in the story was the statement in 4:17, "Repent, for the kingdom of heaven is at hand," when the fishermen drop everything to follow Jesus, the story indicates that they *may* have understood the command to repent. The four followers represent an ideal at this point in the story; they indicate the kind of person Jesus is seeking. As a result, the followers are presented in a very positive light. Their response to Jesus' request and promise serves as a general characterization that can be viewed by the T-CR, at this first presentation, as something awaiting more thorough developments.

The context, therefore, contains information made available to the T-CR about Jesus as the Son of God, who lives and acts in direct response to the Father's will and is further identified, in a general way, in the thesis statement about the future kingdom. But Jesus' mission, unlike John the Baptist's, also involves the choice of a group of followers. It is possible, then, because of the proximity of the summary teaching (4:17) stated in the verse immediately preceding incident one, that the action of the four fishermen in following Jesus could be recognized as the proper way to respond to the thesis statement, the command to repent.

Summary

How has the T-CR been informed about the followers?

Jesus asks two pairs of brothers, fishermen, to "come after" him so that they may become "fishers of people." Jesus' use of a metaphor as a means of stating the rationale for following him raises a question about its exact meaning — something that is not yet clarified and may be clarified by later incidents in the story. The "followers" seem to have understood the metaphor, an indication of their possible comprehension and of their interests. *What* they thought it meant is not stated but the context informs the T-CR what Jesus expects of followers.

The immediate response of the brothers implies their high interest in such a future and their positive evaluation of Jesus, of his status as someone worth following and of his capability to make them "fishers of people." Their understanding and knowledge about Jesus is not stated, but the context provides the T-CR with a large amount of information about Jesus' high status, authority, and reliability. First, Jesus fits into God's overall program, as shown in the genealogy and the fulfillment quotations. Second, his status, authority, and reliability have been recognized by a prophet-like and God-influenced individual, John the Baptist. Third, he is also acknowledged as the Son of God by the anti-Father supernatural being, Satan. Fourth, Jesus' own understanding of his task, stated in the same words as those used by John the Baptist, the respectful prophet, gives the T-CR a specific context for understanding the implications of Jesus' request — that these four men will repent because the kingdom is at hand. The response of the four fishermen is thus presented as a positive reaction in this narrative world. It gives the word "follow" a positive meaning. A follower is someone who responds positively to Jesus' message. Most important is that the task or goal of the followers, which they accept, is to become "fishers of people."

From the point of view of the narrative method, the characterization of the disciples is, for the T-CR, an awareness of the need to comprehend the metaphorical image. Although the meaning of the phrase "fishers of people" is a gap for the T-CR, its meaning can be expected to expand as the story continues.

Character-Shaping Incident Two:

THE STILLING OF THE STORM
Matt. 8:18–27

I NCIDENT ONE was the introduction of the "followers" as a feature
in the world of Matthew's story. Incident two is the first occurrence
of a more detailed interaction in which the T-CR receives specific
information about the incident itself and the reaction of the followers
to Jesus. As the chart of incident two shows, this incident in chapter 8,
about one-fourth of the way through the story, is only the second occurrence in Matthew's story in which the narrator reports a response
by the followers/disciples to an action or words of Jesus. The long section of teaching on the mountain (5:3–7:27) that precedes it is directed
to the "disciples," the first time this word is used (5:1). Although Jesus
addressed the disciples as he taught, there had been no report of any
response by the "followers" until this incident on the lake.

Details of Event

The T-CR is clearly informed of the disciples as characters when they
awaken Jesus to plead for help and, as a result, are criticized by Jesus.
The incident concludes with the narrator quoting their uncertainty about
who Jesus is.

> [18]Now when Jesus saw great crowds around him, he gave orders
> to go over to the other side. [19]And a scribe came up and said to
> him, "Teacher, I will follow you wherever you go." [20]And Jesus
> said to him, "Foxes have holes, and birds of the air have nests; but
> the Son of Man has nowhere to lay his head." [21]Another of the
> disciples said to him, "Lord, let me first go and bury my father."
> [22]But Jesus said to him, "Follow me, and leave the dead to bury
> their own dead." [23]And when he got into the boat, his disciples
> followed him. [24]And behold, there arose a great storm on the sea,
> so that the boat was being swamped by the waves; but he was
> asleep. [25]And they went and woke him, saying, "Save, Lord; we are
> perishing." [26]And he said to them, "Why are you afraid, O men of

Disciple Character-Shaping Analysis #2: Matthew 8:23–27
Expanded Section: Matthew 4:23–9:8

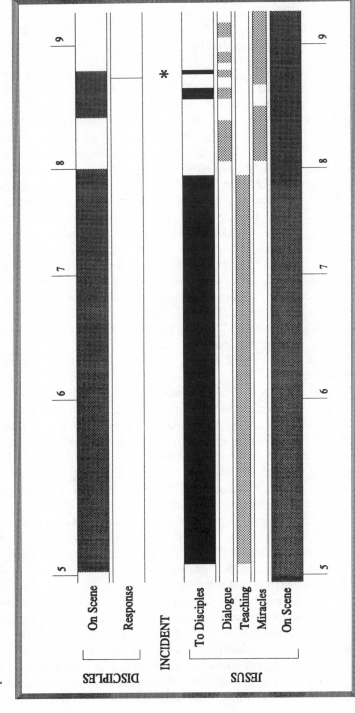

little faith?" Then he rose and rebuked the winds and the sea; and there was a great calm. [27]And the men marveled, saying, "What sort of man is this, that even winds and sea obey him?"

This incident is sometimes listed as two incidents: (1) the story of the stilling of the storm (8:18, 23–27); and (2) Jesus' response to two statements from potential followers (8:19–22). However, as part of Matthew's story, it is one incident because it begins by referring to the boat trip. The narrator reports that Jesus "orders" the disciples to go to the other side of the lake (8:18). But before there is any indication of their response, the narrator reports that a scribe affirms that he will follow Jesus wherever he goes (8:19). Jesus responds with the metaphorical proverb about foxes and birds having resting places which the Son of Man does not have (8:20). This immediate juxtaposition informs the T-CR (1) that this exchange is occasioned by the order to go to the other side; and (2) that Jesus implies that it will not be easy to follow him. The next sentence (8:21) reports that "another of the disciples" asks to be excused to bury his father, implying that the previous speaker, the scribe, was also a follower of Jesus. Jesus' response, about letting the dead bury the dead (8:22), helps clarify that the implication of the proverb about the foxes and birds is indeed correct: following Jesus requires absolute, immediate commitment.

In the next verse (8:23) the narrator states that the disciples "followed him" into the boat, an action that informs the T-CR that the disciples are obedient, a confirmation of the previous character-shaping incident. Although it is not clearly stated, the T-CR is informed in a limited way that the ones who questioned Jesus are part of this group of disciples, who have been associated with those who follow. They are distinct from the crowd but their number, names, and characteristics have not been stated up to this point. The word "follow" has been used prior to this incident to characterize the four fishermen, the "crowd" (4:25; 8:1), and the crowd by implication ("those who followed," 8:10). It is only the four fishermen who have been described as ones who "follow" in response to a specific order or request of Jesus (4:20, 22). Thus the T-CR has been informed about the positive action of following.

The importance of the incident for adding to the T-CR's understanding of the disciples, however, lies primarily in the narrator's depiction of their actions and related statement. They awaken Jesus, when the boat is being swamped, with the demand, "Save, Lord. We are perishing" (8:25). This indicates that they are fearful about their safety. Yet, at the same time, they realize that Jesus, the Lord, can do something to protect them. That Jesus could sleep indicates that such a difficult situation does not affect him as it does the disciples. Therefore, the disciples are presented as responding in an understandable manner but, in contrast,

Jesus' reaction seems extreme: "Why are you afraid, O men of little faith?" (8:26). Although the narrator describes the situation so that it is not *un*reasonable to expect them to be worried, Jesus castigates them for being afraid and dubs them as "men of little faith." The T-CR is thus brought to question the rationale of Jesus' response. Jesus' immediate action, however, shows the T-CR exactly what the disciples, being "afraid," did not understand: Jesus is able to calm the storm by rebuking the winds and sea. "The men" in the boat are then described by the narrator as marveling (8:27). They ask, "What sort of man is this, that even the winds and sea obey him?"

It is clear, then, that the disciples do not comprehend Jesus' authority and power. When Jesus calls them "men of little faith," the T-CR is informed that this is Jesus' evaluation of their response to what they considered a life-threatening situation. They ask him to save them, which indicates they know that he could do it. They are impressed but uncertain. Nevertheless, Jesus expected them to recognize his authority, but they have not made much progress toward being fully committed followers. Thus the phrase "men of little faith" now has a specific connotation for the T-CR: to be a disciple is to be more than just someone obeying Jesus or following him closely as he moves around Galilee. The traits that the T-CR can associate with the disciples, because of this incident, are both positive and negative: obedient — they obey the command of Jesus to travel with him to the other side of the lake; limited comprehension — they lack complete understanding and certainty, which Jesus criticizes. They are afraid because they do not recognize his ability to handle such incidents.

This is the first time in Matthew's story that the disciples speak; it is an event different from the simple obedience and apparent comprehension depicted in incident one, the call of the four fishermen. Here the narrator gives more elaborate detail about the disciples' role in the story, and the T-CR has now received more detail about the complexity of their response to Jesus. The initial positive impression from incident one is now being modified. Therefore, it is necessary to examine the context, the material that precedes this incident, to see what further information the T-CR might attach to the disciples' behavior.

Context

The upper portion of the expanded section of chart two illustrates that the disciples have been "on scene" since the call of the four fishermen, but in a passive way. They are listeners, the addressees (5:1–2) of the teaching on the mountain, which is specifically directed to them. After the speech, when the narrator reports that the crowd was also part of the audience (7:28), the story focuses on miracles, with emphasis on the importance of dialogue with Jesus.

Although the word "disciple" was not used in the calling of Peter, Andrew, James, and John, it is associated with them when first used in 5:1, where the narrator reports that when Jesus went up on the mountain and sat down, "His disciples (learners) came to him." This description informs the T-CR that some of the crowd came to Jesus because they are interested in following him and, in addition, want to be educated by Jesus, perhaps to learn how to be a fisher of people, which Peter, Andrew, James, and John were very interested in seeking. Since the word "follow," which was associated with the four fishermen, has also been used to describe the crowd, the T-CR is guided to look favorably upon the crowd.

The speech in chapters 5–7, the teaching on the mountain, is addressed to the disciples: "Seeing the crowd, he went up on the mountain, and when he sat down his disciples came to him. And he opened his mouth and taught them, saying..." (5:1–2). The crowd is mentioned as the reason for Jesus going to the mountain, but it is the disciples who are said to have come to him. The T-CR is informed, then, that the term "disciples" is either another word for the crowd or a group from among the crowd. Since the word "follow" is not used, it is not certain whether "disciples" refers to the four fishermen. Thus, the T-CR is not clearly informed exactly which individuals are now being taught by Jesus.

What impact does a speech, such as this teaching on the mountain, have on the T-CR's comprehension of the disciples' character? If they are the only addressees, or at least part of a larger audience, the way in which they could be instructed must be considered. Since Jesus had already said to the four fishermen that he would make them "fishers of people" (4:19), the T-CR can anticipate that a speech addressed to "disciples" would train the followers and explain what it means to be a "fisher of people," especially when it is introduced with the phrase: "He taught them" (5:2). What does Jesus expect from those who are following him?

The most obvious educational material would be those statements directly addressed to the audience, the disciples. That the instruction is specifically directed at the disciples is clear because there are a significant number of second-person pronouns in the speech. For example: "Blessed are *you* when..." (5:11); "*You* are the salt of the earth" (5:13); "Thus, when *you* give alms..." (6:2). The T-CR, who has been informed of Jesus' high status and authority, is now informed how Jesus clarifies what he expects of the disciples, by implication, what he assumes they can comprehend.

The organization or structure of the sayings quoted in the teaching on the mountain has been debated by exegetes for a long time. Our focus here is to view it as part of Matthew's narrative, especially as a factor in influencing the T-CR about Jesus' expectations of the disciples. As a result, I will not deal with every aspect of the speech, but rather focus on those elements that are significant for understanding the characterization of the disciples.

The teaching begins with statements describing those who are "blessed" (5:3–12). The first eight blessings are stated as applying to a group of people: "Blessed are the poor in spirit," or "those who mourn." In the ninth blessing (5:11), however, the disciples are addressed more directly ("Blessed are *you*") with the same emphasis on blessing, thereby implying that Jesus' earlier statements were also intended for the disciples' education. This arrangement of material — the use of an indefinite addressee followed later by the specification of the disciples — informs the T-CR that the standards stated in the blessings apply to *any follower.* The ninth blessing is not only addressed to the disciples, but also refers to more specific situations. "You," the disciples, are described as reviled, persecuted, and accused of evil because of Jesus ("on my account," 5:11).

It is also important to note that the blessedness is projected toward the future. Just as Jesus had preached, "Repent, for the kingdom of heaven *is at hand,*" he now states that the blessedness the disciples have received is the promise that they *will be* rewarded "in heaven." Furthermore, Jesus draws a comparison between the disciples and the prophets of the past (5:12), a correlation between the present situation and past actions of the Father, similar to the use of fulfillment quotations so prominent in the framework. As a result, the T-CR receives a clear indication of the purpose of the speech: the disciples are being informed of the standards against which they will be measured. Throughout the speech, the T-CR is guided to expect a clear picture of Jesus' expectations of a disciple, unless something contradicts this assumption.

After an opening in which the disciples are clearly addressed in the blessings (5:3–11), the speech continues to focus on them with the frequent use of "you." In addition, there are many commands within the speech in which Jesus details what he expects from them.

After the blessings inform the disciples of things to anticipate in the future, Jesus next describes them as the salt of the earth (5:13) and the light of the world (5:14–16), a use of metaphor similar to when he asked the four fishermen to follow him. Understood as the salt of the earth, the disciples would be useless if they lost their saltiness, their ability to do what is expected of them. As the light of the world, they would fall below their expected level if they did not perform the good works that would enable others to glorify the Father.

After this beginning, Jesus advises the disciples about how he expects them to judge his mission: "Do not think that I have come to abolish the law and the prophets" (5:17). This is followed by a statement about the authority of the Torah (5:18) which ends with a demand that the disciples' actions should exceed that of the Pharisees in quality. The following six examples (antitheses) of Jesus' understanding of the law inform the T-CR of the importance and meaning of the word "fulfill" for Jesus (5:21–48). They supply guidelines for the disciples to comprehend how their behavior could exceed the righteousness of the Pharisees. The second-person form of address continues in this part of the speech, and the examples end with a final command: "You, therefore, must be perfect, as your heavenly father is perfect" (5:48). Jesus is portrayed as someone who explains his high acceptance of the tradition (law and prophets) with a broader, more everyday applicability. Commands directed at the disciples, which begin to illustrate his expectations, are based on a careful understanding of certain elements of the law and prophets. Thus, the T-CR is informed of Jesus' high expectation of the disciples in this first section of the speech.

The examples of required action continue in the next portion of the speech with a different focus — the misuse of piety: "Beware of practicing *your* piety before men...." Each of the three examples (giving alms, praying, and fasting) continues to be directly addressed to the disciples (6:1–18). Jesus continues to show how a true follower/disciple is expected to act. The Father's expectations are being clarified, and such examples help the T-CR gain information about what is expected. Pious action, such as prayer, is emphasized for the reason it is performed: the connection between piety (alms, prayer, fasting) and perfection is based on the follower's purpose for performing it.

The next section of the speech does not appear to be organized by topics. Nevertheless, it does continue to express Jesus' expectations of the disciples, combining commands and examples/metaphors. The heavy use of metaphors gives the T-CR less precise information and will require more specific information as the story progresses to find the appropriate meanings. In addition, the references to God or Father add more specific context to help clarify, for the T-CR, the basis for identifying positive action. The disciples are told:

- Do not lay up treasure on the earth but in heaven. (6:19–21)

- The eye is a lamp and therefore darkness represents imperfection. (6:22–23)

- No one can serve two masters — God and Mammon. (6:24)

- Do not be anxious. (6:25–34)

Using natural items from the world, such as birds, lilies, food, and clothing, Jesus focuses on the Father as the source of life. It is in this pericope that Jesus uses the phrase "men of little faith" for the first time, and therefore the T-CR is informed that faith is the opposite of anxiety. What it means to be men of little faith is not clearly expressed at this point in the story. What Jesus expects of the disciples is further clarified however when Jesus, near the conclusion of this pericope, asks them to "seek first his kingdom."

- Judge not. Why do you see the speck? Jesus is opposed to anyone who overlooks the most obvious features of a situation. (7:1–5)

- Do not give dogs what is holy. Be sure you know the situation before you give a quick response. (7:6)

- Ask and it will be given to you. Use the Father as a guide. The Father in heaven will act as a responsive, sensible individual. (7:7–11)

- "Whatever you wish that people would do to you" is a way of knowing what you should do, because it is in line with the law and the prophets. (7:12)

- Enter by the narrow gate, that is, by perfection. The wide gate, the easy way, leads to destruction. (7:13–14)

- Beware of false prophets; they come as sheep but really are wolves. A good tree cannot bear evil fruit. As a follower, you will have ability to look beyond the way people present themselves, that is, you will know them by their fruit. (7:15–20)

- "Not everyone who says to me, 'Lord, Lord,' shall enter the kingdom of heaven." Although not a metaphor, it reemphasizes that the one who does the will of the Father is being a proper "follower" (7:21–23).

This teaching on the mountain concludes with a story of the builders of two houses, one built on sand and one on rock (7:24–27). The house that is not destroyed by a flood, because it is founded on the rock, represents the person who does not merely listen to Jesus' words but who "does them," while the house on the sand that falls represents those who listen to the words but do "not do them." The comparison focuses not on listening to, but on obeying, "these words of mine." As the conclusion to the teaching, which is a lengthy and specific set of details about what Jesus expects of his followers/disciples, this metaphor is not only a "guide to perfection" for those who seek to be an acceptable follower/ disciple, but emphasizes that the speech did not merely intend to inform the T-CR about Jesus' understanding of himself or his career. The story of the two houses reminds the T-CR of the purpose of the speech: it is intended as a set of guidelines for the disciples. Also, by making use of metaphors, it requires the T-CR to continue to look for incidents which would help clarify and specify the metaphor's meaning.

The narrator's comments about the speech (7:28–29) add a detail not indicated at the beginning — that the crowds were present and listening. The narrator says they were astonished because of Jesus' authority, which is unlike that of the scribes. This report about the presence and thoughts of the crowds informs the T-CR that although the teaching was addressed to the *disciples,* it was also heard by the crowds, those mentioned at the start of the speech as the reason for Jesus' decision to go up on the mountain (5:1). Thus he was not going to escape the crowds; they are not portrayed in a negative way. And the word "disciple" is used at this point in the narrative as a term which applies to any follower. The mention of Jesus' authority in teaching also informs the T-CR that the crowd views him as someone similar to the scribes but as one who stands above them. Since the T-CR has received significant information in the framework of the story, the statement about Jesus' status over the scribes is based on the direct correlation between Jesus and the Father.

The importance of this statement by the narrator, at the conclusion of Jesus' lengthy teaching, lies partially in its way of informing the T-CR by relating previous deeds and traits to the immediate situation, that is, by incorporating all the relevant information from the framework. Any follower of Jesus is expected to act in a positive way toward the Father since Jesus is the son of God. The T-CR thus has been informed of the high level of Jesus' expectations for the disciples and what it is based on.

After the conclusion of the teaching, there are three incidents in which Jesus, the speaker, is portrayed as one who moves among the people and responds to their requests and problems (8:1–16). The disciples are not mentioned in any of these incidents, but there is no direct or indirect indication that they have left the scene. The T-CR is informed that they did accompany Jesus in character-shaping incident two, the stilling of the storm, which begins at 8:18.

In the first of these three incidents (8:1–4), a leper is cleansed when Jesus responds to the leper's confident request for help. When Jesus commands the leper to follow the legal requirements associated with the verification of the cleansing, it is a clear demonstration of Jesus' previously stated respect for upholding the rules of the Torah (5:17–20); he has come to fulfill the law, not abolish it.

The second of these incidents reports Jesus' astonishment about the "faith" demonstrated by a Gentile centurion (8:5–13). Although his faith is not defined or described by the narrator, it is presented to the T-CR in the centurion's speech when he explains why he is confident of Jesus' ability to heal his servant without entering a Gentile's house. The T-CR has not been given much information about "faith"; the word had not been used previously except in Jesus' teaching on the mountain, where he addresses the disciples as men of "little faith" (6:30). In that context, those of "little faith" are those anxious for their life and those who do not acknowledge what God the Father can do. They should "seek first his kingdom and righteousness" (6:33). Thus "little faith" correlates with being anxious about what God can do for a human being. To understand the faith of the centurion, the T-CR is informed of the centurion's recognition of Jesus' "authority," which the centurion says he understands and which was also used by the narrator in describing the crowd's positive reaction to the teaching on the mountain. The T-CR has received limited information about the word "faith" — but both the little faith of the disciples and the centurion's recognition of Jesus' authority connect it with an affirmation of Jesus' status. Thus the T-CR is informed not only of Jesus' high expectations of the disciples, in Jesus' teaching on the mountain, but is shown a contrasting character, a Gentile, whom Jesus declares a positive individual when he recognizes Jesus as someone who can act on the Father's behalf. To help understand the little faith of the disciples, the T-CR is shown the faith of the centurion.

The third incident is a brief report of Jesus' healing of Peter's mother-in-law (8:14–15) followed by a summary statement of exorcisms and healings of "all who were ill" (8:16). This helps underline for the T-CR the accuracy of the centurion's faith, that is, that Jesus has the authority to heal.

The point that must be emphasized, therefore, in light of the context of incident two, is that it helps explain the meaning of Jesus' criticism of the disciples as "men of little faith" (8:26). Because the word "faith" is first used in a *positive* way at 8:10, where faith is given meaning when Jesus responds to the centurion's confidence about his ability to heal, it sets a definite context for the incident that focuses on the disciples. In the stilling of the storm, therefore, he is criticizing the disciples because of their limited faith. Although they are adequate enough to follow him and to listen to his interpretation of the law, their faith is not strong enough in this dangerous situation to enable them to have the kind of confidence exhibited by the centurion.

Immediate Context

The last section (8:16–17) of the context, which immediately precedes character-shaping incident two, the story of the stilling of the storm (8:18–26), is a summary statement and a fulfillment quotation from the narrator, the format that has been so prominent in the framework (1:22–23; 2:5–6; 2:15; 2:17–18; 2:23; 4:14–16). The narrator has earlier informed the T-CR of the relationship between current events and the records of God's statements. The action of Jesus as a healer is a fulfillment of the previous sentence (8:16), which is a broad summary statement about Jesus' healing ability. The combination of these two sentences changes the flow of the narrative from a report about interactions between Jesus and specific individuals, to a comment about the correlation between Jesus' deeds and the written record of the Father's previous statements. As a result, the T-CR is encouraged to combine (1) the principle of recognizing the way various events in the life of Jesus are directly related to statements or predictions contained in the earlier spoken material with (2) the way in which Jesus has claimed to be fulfilling the law and prophets both by what he says and by what he does.

Summary

Prior to this disciple character-shaping incident (two), the T-CR had been given no character-shaping information about the disciples and a very limited, but possibly positive, view of the four followers who are to become the "fishers of people." Since the phrase is not explained, the T-CR requires more information to understand what it means to become a fisher of people. When the word "disciples" is first used, they are reported to come to Jesus and he teaches them in detail about what he expects of them. Thus with the heavy focus on the high status of Jesus as the son of God, in the context of this incident the T-CR now receives Jesus' specific expectations of disciples, and perhaps also of followers. These expectations are very important for the T-CR in this narrative world.

Jesus often states in his teaching of the disciples that, although they should act and behave in ways that meet the Father's law, they are likely to perform at a low level and can be expected to fall short of his expectations. It is the will of the Father that is the way of understanding whether they have been "perfect" or not. It is a combination of guidelines and limitations. The T-CR is informed of what the disciples *ought* to be and what they are *likely* to be.

After the disciples received Jesus' expectations, the T-CR is shown a character, the centurion, who is judged by the high-expecting Jesus as one who has faith, the recognition of authority.

Given this context, this incident is important in understanding the disciples because the T-CR receives a report of a specific, detailed response on their part after having been told of Jesus' expectations. The disciples are presented as followers respectful enough to ask for Jesus' help when the storm threatens the boat. But Jesus' response makes it clear that their request demonstrates to him that they do not recognize the authority which he possesses. And their response to Jesus' miraculous action in calming the storm makes it clear that they do not, as yet, comprehend "what sort of man" he is. They are portrayed as truly different from the centurion.

In addition, to have a scribe say "I will follow you," and another disciple explain why he will not follow every day, brings to the T-CR's foreground the report that Jesus had received a positive response from the four fishermen who were requested to follow him in order to become "fishers of people." The word "disciple" has not been defined in this narrative world as yet. Although Jesus' two comments at the beginning of the incident seem to imply that the role will require dedication to the one followed, the T-CR has not yet been informed of how the disciples are meeting Jesus' expectations. Since the T-CR has been informed of Jesus' education of the disciples, who are apparently similar to the followers, it is clear that the question will be raised about whether they actually are able to act as Jesus expects.

The T-CR is also informed that Jesus' criticism of their request for help shows that they are, in part, what he anticipated: people of little faith. As true followers of Jesus, they should not be afraid even though they are in a dangerous situation. The T-CR, as yet, has not received a clear definition of the term "fear," other than to know that Jesus considers it an inadequate response. Since the T-CR has received extensive information about the origin and authority of Jesus, it is clear that the disciples have not, as yet, been able to reach a similar comprehension of the close relation between Jesus and the Father.

The characterization of the disciples has not been detailed previously because the T-CR must first be given an elaborate indication of what is expected of them. Although Jesus expects a strong response from them, he also informs them that they will not meet this expectation: to be blessed could also mean that they will be persecuted; they will be anxious even though they should not be. The will of the Father is the primary requirement for a proper follower/disciple. Thus, when they do not meet Jesus' expectations in this situation, they are not being presented as a group of opponents but as "limited" followers.

Thus the T-CR has been informed about the importance of disciples as followers, but also about their inability to meet the high level of faith that Jesus would appreciate. They are recognized by Jesus, when they are portrayed in some detail, as people of *little* faith rather than *no* faith. Whether they will be able to meet Jesus' high expectations remains to be seen.

Character-Shaping Incident Three:

THE DISCIPLES' AFFIRMATIVE RESPONSE TO THE PARABLES
Matt. 13:51–52

A S THE EXPANDED SECTION (8:28–13:58) of the chart for incident three clearly displays, in this portion of the story Jesus directs a significant number of actions to the disciples: miracles in chapter 9, teaching in chapter 10, and dialogue in chapter 13. Although the disciples are not "on scene" throughout, there are four responses that the narrator reports. The fourth response, a reply to Jesus' question (14:51), is a character-shaping incident. The previous three are not character-shaping because the T-CR is not given enough information about the actions reported. The first response is "Matthew's" acceptance of his call (9:9); the second response is a question the disciples ask about why Jesus speaks in parables (13:10); the third response is a request for an explanation of a parable (13:36).

Details of Event

This incident is very short, including the disciples' reply to Jesus' question about his just-completed teaching and then concluding with Jesus' reaction to their reply. It has a clear character-shaping property.

> [51] "Have you understood all this?" They said to him, "Yes." [52] And he said to them, "Therefore every scribe who has been trained [*matheteutheis*] for the kingdom of heaven is like a householder who brings out of his treasure what is new and what is old."

This incident is considered a disciple character-shaping event for two reasons. First, it reports a precise statement by the disciples to a direct question from Jesus: the narrator reports that they answer, "Yes," when Jesus asks them, "Have you understood all this?" Second, it reports Jesus' response to their affirmation, even though the narrator does not supply explicit, "omniscient" information about Jesus' reply. Since

Disciple Character-Shaping Analysis #3: Matthew 13:51–52
Expanded Section: Matthew 8:28–13:58

there is no indication from the narrator that the disciples are or are not sincere, Jesus' reply to their affirmation is the only way to comprehend its meaning. The narrator reports that Jesus said, "Therefore every scribe who has been trained for the kingdom of heaven is like a householder who brings out of his treasure what is new and what is old."

Jesus' response does not indicate any skepticism or unacceptance but, rather, implies acceptance of their claim to have understood his parables. Because his response begins with "therefore" (*dia touto*), the T-CR is guided to accept (1) that Jesus is, of course, responding to their answer; and (2) that he recognizes the implications of their affirmative response. Jesus' metaphor (simile) compares those "scribes," who have been "trained" or "discipled" for the kingdom, with householders who bring both new and old from their treasure. There have been many attempts to identify what specifically are the new and old items in this metaphor. For the moment, it is enough to note the importance of the verb *matheteutheis* (trained), which comes from the same root as the noun "disciple" (*mathetes*). Thus, because of the limited information about Jesus' attitude and his meaning in the metaphor, Jesus is presented by the narrator as recognizing the implications of the disciples' answer, but not necessarily whether the disciples' affirmation is true. His response informs the disciples of the quality or character of their task by using a metaphoric statement, similar to the parables just presented to them, and in full agreement with their assertion of having understood the parables; that is, if they understood the parables, they should be able to understand the comparison in his response. Whether they have actually understood the parables or not has not been revealed to the T-CR.

Thus, based on the incident itself, the T-CR receives a clear indication of the disciples as characters. They view themselves as followers of Jesus who claim that they comprehend his teaching in parables. They are confident about their ability to grasp the meaning of Jesus' metaphorical message. Jesus' use of *another* metaphor to express the implications of their response helps to emphasize the importance of their capability to understand. As the story continues there may be an indication of the validity of their affirmation.

Since their response refers to what Jesus had just taught, the context of this incident is especially important.

Context

Just how this response will be understood by the T-CR must now be examined by looking at the preceding narrative. There is a large amount of material between this character-shaping incident (13:51–2) and the previous one (8:18–27). Using narrative categories, it can be divided into five sections, based on the flow of the story and its references to the disciples.

Section A (8:28–9:35) immediately follows the disciples' reaction to Jesus' calming of the sea. It is best described as the response of different individuals to Jesus, the healer. In this section, the disciples are only mentioned once: in 9:10, where they are eating with Jesus at "Matthew's" table.

Section B (10:1–42) is Jesus' teaching of the disciples. The speech (10:5–42), preceded by the naming of the twelve (10:1–4), is addressed to the twelve "apostles" and describes not only their task as apostles but the kinds of reaction they can expect when they act as apostles.

Section C (11:1–30) focuses primarily on the response to Jesus' "deeds." After Jesus' response to John the Baptist's disciples' question about Jesus' status, Jesus portrays John the Baptist in a positive way. This is followed by different levels of opposition to Jesus, and chapter 11 ends with Jesus repeating the general request: "Come to me." The disciples are never mentioned as present in these incidents.

Section D (12:1–45) describes the debates Jesus has with various individuals and groups. The disciples reappear in chapter 12 but with little involvement. Chapter 12 concludes with a reference to the disciples when Jesus contrasts his kin with those who do the will of his Father (12:46–50).

Section E (13:1–50), the immediate context for character-shaping incident three, begins with an emphasis on the crowd being taught in parables (13:2). After Jesus presents the parable of the sower, the disciples respond by asking about this mode of teaching (13:10). Jesus' reply contains more parables and two interpretations.

Section A (8:28–9:35): After Jesus' criticism of the disciples in character-shaping incident two, when they do not recognize his authority to control the sea, the narrator continues to focus on Jesus' power and authority over demons and, especially, the various reactions to these demonstrations of power. He exorcises the legion of demons but the people of Gadarene beg him to leave (8:28–34); he heals the paralytic in his own city and the crowds glorify God because of Jesus' authority (9:1–8). The call of Matthew and the meal at his house (9:9–13) result in Jesus defining his mission as one for sinners, thereby emphasizing that it is open for any follower, including the disciples.

The dialogue incident, between Jesus and John the Baptist's disciples (9:14–17), begins with their question about Jesus' disciples' lack of fasting. It continues the trend in this part of the narrative of putting more emphasis on the interaction between Jesus and the people and less on the miracles as such. But the question is about why the requirements placed on Jesus' disciples differ from those placed on John's disciples and the Pharisees (9:14). Jesus' answer emphasizes the distinctiveness and limited nature of the present time, which should be kept distinct from the future which will be different (9:15). He concludes with more metaphors: a used garment is torn and old wineskins are destroyed when the significance of unshrunken cloth or new wine is not properly recognized (9:16–17). The final statement, "and so both (wine and wineskins) are preserved," seems to summarize Jesus' point. That requirements, such as fasting, are *not* placed on his disciples indicates the distinctiveness of Jesus' presence. The T-CR is thereby encouraged to consider Jesus' disciples as a distinct and significant group. Their distinctiveness and possible importance is suggested. Thus, in an indirect way, the issue of the disciples is foregrounded for the T-CR in the midst of a series of miracles that emphasize how various individuals respond to demonstrations of Jesus' power and authority. This raises the question of the comparison of the disciples as characters with other characters in the story.

The final three healings in section A continue to emphasize both Jesus' authority and the response of the recipients. In the first miracle (9:18–26), while Jesus is on the way to heal the ruler's daughter (9:19), the woman with the hemorrhage who touches his garment is described *by Jesus* as someone whose faith has made her well (9:20–22), thereby giving the T-CR a clear indication of the kind of action and attitude that Jesus values highly. This is the second time Jesus has used the word "faith" in a positive way, and yet the T-CR has not received detailed information about it. The disciples are mentioned as following Jesus to the ruler's house (9:19), and as a result they can be considered witnesses to the astonishment expressed by those who see what power he possesses. Although not very specific, the action of the woman helps clarify the disciples' need for faith just as the centurion's faith had also contrasted with disciples, who had been called "men of little faith."

In the second event (9:27–31), the two blind men are healed because they acknowledge that they believe Jesus is able to cure them; once again, the T-CR is informed of a proper response to Jesus.

In the third event (9:32–34), the healing of the dumb-demoniac, the miracle is briefly described. Then the narrator states that the crowds are impressed, and they are quoted as saying that they have never seen such power in Israel. The Pharisees, in contrast, are quoted as ascribing his healing power to Beelzebub, that is, Jesus' power or authority is not from the Father. The T-CR had been informed of the Pharisees four times previously: (1) John the Baptist's speech is a criticism of the Pharisees and shows how critical he is of them (3:7–12). (2) In Jesus' first speech (5:3–7:27), which expressed his expectations of the disciples, he stated that he considers the righteousness of the scribes and Pharisees so inadequate that they will not enter the kingdom. (3) The Pharisees were presented negatively when the narrator reported in 9:11 that they asked Jesus' disciples why Jesus eats with people which they, the Pharisees, consider inappropriate. (4) The criticism of the Pharisees was also expressed when John the Baptist's disciples asked Jesus why "we," the disciples of John and the Pharisees, find certain activity required but Jesus does not require it of his followers (9:14). Thus the T-CR has been given a specific or implied negative image of the Pharisees. Now that they are again contrasted with the followers, the T-CR has been led to see the Pharisees as critics of Jesus. Incidents in such close proximity, and witnessed by the disciples, help define clearly Jesus' (and the narrator's) image of a truly proper follower and a contrasting opponent.

In the conclusion of section A (9:35–38), after a summary of Jesus' activity the narrator states that Jesus is compassionate toward the crowd. The reason for Jesus' compassion is then explained with a metaphor which asserts that the people are harassed and helpless, like sheep without a shepherd. With the T-CR informed about the state of Jesus' mind, the narrator reports Jesus telling the disciples that the harvest is plentiful, the laborers few, and requests that they pray to the Lord for laborers (9:37–38). It is another instance in which Jesus uses metaphorical language to communicate his understanding of the situation to his disciples. By mentioning the disciples in the summary as those addressed by Jesus (9:37), the narrator indicates to the T-CR that the disciples should be qualified followers and are to be recognized as on-the-spot witnesses who should be incorporating the lessons contained in these events. Such followers are an integral part of Jesus', and the Father's, program.

Section B (10:1–42): Having addressed the disciples using the metaphor of the harvest and its need for laborers, Jesus' focus on the disciples continues when section B begins with a listing of the twelve disciples. The disciples are also called "apostles" (those sent out) and told to go to the lost sheep of the house of Israel, a clear indication that Jesus conceives of them as the laborers he had just mentioned who would be needed to assist those who are harassed and helpless.

In Matthew 10:1, the phrase "*twelve* disciples" is used for the first time; it is used here without further explanation. The T-CR is given the names of the Twelve. Only five of this group of twelve have been previously named, although many different individuals, as well as the crowd, have been described as followers. When in 10:2 they are referred to as "twelve *apostles*" (those "sent out"), the narrator is focusing on the smaller group. Since the word "apostle" had not been used previously in Matthew's story, for the T-CR its significance could only be based on Jesus' expectation and may be defined by the teaching that follows. Within the list of the twelve apostles, Judas Iscariot is described as the one who betrayed Jesus. Since there is no incident about Judas up to this point in the story which is identifiable, and no other indication of what the information might mean, the T-CR has a "gap" and is led to anticipate a negative tendency from this disciple. Since the information is stated by the narrator, some action in the future is anticipated, and the T-CR is required to raise questions about the reliability of the disciples and their capacity to act as Jesus expects. The last of the chosen disciples is thereby described in terms of an action, but for the T-CR it is not clear what betrayal represents. It is apparently negative, but it is not obvious and could only be clarified by some future incident or action.

The narrator introduces the speech directed to the disciples (10:5–42) by stating that Jesus sent them out (using the verb ἀποστελλω to reflect the term "apostle") and "charged them," in other words, commanded them. The narrator thereby gives the T-CR a specific indication of what Jesus *requires* of the disciples beyond the details of the first speech. This speech begins with Jesus' command of where to go, that is, to the lost sheep of the house of Israel. The preaching they should perform ("the kingdom of God is at hand") is a message similar to the thesis with which he began his ministry in 4:17, except that Jesus does not tell them to begin with the command to repent as had both John the Baptist and Jesus in their references to the coming of the kingdom. They are also told to heal, to raise the dead, to cleanse lepers, and to cast out demons. The speech is important because the T-CR receives more details about Jesus' expectations of how the disciples should perform as "fishers of people." The first teaching, in chapters 5–7, focused on what they should be like. This teaching moves a step further by clarifying what Jesus expects them to do, what it means to be an apostle.

This speech, therefore, elaborates Jesus' expectations for the disciples and provides a clear guide for the T-CR about how the disciples' actions will be judged. It has three main sections and a conclusion. In the first section, Jesus informs the disciples about:

1. What they should do: go (10:5), preach (10:7), and heal (10:8).

2. How they should live when on the mission: accept no pay (10:8–9), take no extra clothes (10:10), accept hospitality from worthy houses (10:11), and expect some hostile reaction (incorporating a metaphor, 10:13–15).

3. The reactions they will encounter: flogging (10:17), help from the Spirit (10:19–20), inter-family and related troubles (10:21–22).

4. How to respond: avoid direct conflict (10:23) and recognize their close association with Jesus and the negative response it may cause (10:24–25).

Jesus' mention that he might be called Beelzebub reminds the T-CR that the Pharisees had used the term previously (9:34) for someone opposed to the Father.

In the second section of the speech (10:26–39), the disciples are told how to support themselves and how to respond to acceptance or rejection. The emphasis is now a series of *warnings* about the difficulties that they will encounter and the kind of reactions that Jesus anticipates from them. Jesus warns them: beware, do not be anxious, do not fear. The second section also contains a reference to the Father and to Jesus' connection to him (10:32–33) as well as a reference to a cross in connection with the sword (10:34), thereby signaling the trouble that the disciples will confront. This is the first time that *Jesus,* not the narrator, is quoted as using the word "disciple" (10:24–25, 42) and the speech ends with a reference to a follower as a disciple (10:42).

The second section of the speech also contains advice about not being afraid because of the promise of the future (10:26–33) and a more positive statement about the effect of Jesus' presence, that is, the predominance of the sword over peace (10:34–39). It is important that this phrase "do not think" appears only here and in the thesis statement in the previous speech (5:17), and thereby reinforces for the T-CR the emphasis on the disciples and the importance of the word "follow," used just prior to the statement about losing one's life. The focus, then, has moved from warnings about persecution to statements about death (10:38–39).

The speech concludes (10:40–42) with Jesus' emphasis on the close connection between himself and the disciples. He informs the disciples that a person is partially identified by their relation to specific individuals. Thus to be a disciple or follower of Jesus means that one will not lose one's close relation to the Father, the one who sent Jesus.

Section B thus enlarges the T-CR's understanding of the disciples with more specifics of Jesus' expectations. Jesus wants them to obey his initial command to be "apostles" but is obviously concerned about their ability to persevere during negative reactions to their apostolic activity. Up to this point, the T-CR has been informed that Jesus expects the persecution of the disciples, which would begin to indicate to the T-CR some of the possible results of one of the twelve apostles, Judas, being a betrayer.

The use of metaphors continues in Jesus' conversation with the disciples: lost sheep of the house of Israel (10:6), a reference to 9:36; sheep in the midst of wolves, wise as serpents and innocent as doves (10:16); and the analogy of sparrows sold (10:29–31).

Section C (11:1–30): There is a change in narrative flow at the beginning of chapter 11 which leaves a significant gap for the T-CR to complete. The narrator's statement (11:1) following the speech describes it as Jesus "instructing his twelve disciples." The narrator does not say that the disciples did go out, or that they departed to fulfill Jesus' request, but merely that *Jesus* "went on from there to teach and preach in their cities" (11:1). Since the disciples are not mentioned as accompanying Jesus, the T-CR does not know of the disciples' reaction to Jesus' instruction or whether they followed his request to "go to the lost sheep of the house of Israel" (10:6).

The disciples, although not reported "on scene," continue to be important characters for the T-CR when John the Baptist's disciples are mentioned in 11:2. After reporting that Jesus was teaching and preaching, the narrator reports that John the Baptist, who is in prison, questions Jesus by sending his disciples. Should John be considered a disciple as well as someone subservient to Jesus? The distinction between the apparently respondent disciples of Jesus and the uncertainty of John raises the question implied in the earlier section: What is the relationship between John and Jesus? This incident clarifies the distinctiveness of John the Baptist when his disciples ask Jesus: "Are you he who is to come, or shall we look for another?" (11:3). The narrator reports that John the Baptist feels it is necessary to ask such a question when "he heard in prison about the deeds of the Christ" (11:2). Jesus' response is straightforward: tell him what you see and hear, and "blessed is he who takes no offense at me" (11:4–6). Jesus' answer is *not* a criticism of John. And the non-criticism of John continues in the next section (11:7–19) when Jesus stresses the importance of John, to the point of his being called Elijah. Even though the emphasis is on the distinction between John (the preparer) and Jesus (the Son), it is modified in the metaphorical comparison between Jesus and John: one is the reed, the other the prophet (11:7). John's status, as more than a prophet, is verified for the T-CR with another quotation in which John is a Preparer who works for God. In the quotation the emphasis is on "this generation" for their lack of acceptance of either John or Jesus (11:16–19). Jesus' stress on the importance of the *deeds* of wisdom (11:19) informs the T-CR of the connection between Jesus' response and what the narrator reported as John's problem when in prison John heard about the deeds of Christ (11:2). Thus the effect of the passage is positive about John the Baptist, even though John, in prison, questions the appropriateness of Jesus' action.

After showing a positive attitude toward John the Baptist, Jesus "upbraids" places where there is opposition to, or questioning of, his works

(11:20–24). The cities being criticized did not repent in response to Jesus' deeds, as the thesis statement of Jesus (4:17) and John (3:2) commanded. In effect, the T-CR receives examples of the kind of activity that Jesus condemns, that is, the kind he does not expect from the disciples.

Section C concludes with the narrator quoting a saying of Jesus addressed first to the Father ("I thank you," 11:25–26), and second, to the audience ("Come to me . . . ," 11:28). Once again this collection of Jesus' sayings increases the information available to the T-CR about Jesus' expectations. After the intimate relationship between Jesus and the Father is clarified, the concept of coming to Jesus is defined, this time in terms of both its difficulties and its ease.

Section D (12:1–45): Although this unit begins with a phrase similar to the one that introduced the previous paragraph ("At that time"), it initiates an incident which, although it starts with narration, quickly moves to dialogue rather than teaching. The disciples are mentioned at the beginning (12:1) plucking and eating grain on the sabbath. The T-CR's attention is directed toward the disciples because the Pharisees criticize them as those who do what is *not* lawful; in other words, *their* conduct is the basis for the criticism addressed to Jesus (12:2). The emphasis of the incident, however, is clearly on the Pharisees, against whom Jesus speaks in defense of his disciples (12:3–8). The defense is not based on their hunger, however, but on Jesus' presence. The implication for the T-CR is that Jesus accepts the disciples as a group which does indeed recognize his status and authority; that they follow him is again brought to the fore. Since there is no report of the Pharisees' response to Jesus' answer, Jesus' defense of the disciples is indicated as complete.

The emphasis on the conflict between Jesus and the Pharisees continues in the next incident, which concerns healing on the Sabbath (12:9–14). The ending to the incident mentions that the Pharisees simply "went out" and began to plot against Jesus, rather than trying to confront him with another question or to challenge his argument about the appropriateness of the healing on the Sabbath.

When the narrator reports that Jesus withdrew, because he was aware of their opposition ("how to destroy him"), he is accompanied by "many [who] followed him" (12:15). He heals them all and "ordered them not to make him known" (12:15–16). This summary concludes with the fulfillment quotation (12:17–21) from Isaiah regarding the chosen servant upon whom the Spirit rests and who proclaims to the Gentiles. The narrator's use of a fulfillment quotation brings to the foreground, for the T-CR, the authority and power of Jesus which had been carefully stated in the framework of the story. It reaffirms and guides the T-CR to recall the importance of Jesus' connections with the Father, as well as the implication of the importance of the Gentiles. Thus, opposition to Jesus among the religious leaders of the community shows that their rejection of him is in direct opposition to the Father. Those who follow Jesus, including the disciples, are therefore in close relationship with the Father.

The concentration on Jesus' opposition continues in the next incident, 12:22–37, when another healing brings the Pharisees forward, this time with a more precise accusation: "It is only by Beelzebub, the prince of demons, that this man casts out demons" (12:24), a repeat of the accusation made in 9:34. In response, Jesus again uses a variety of metaphors: the problem of a divided kingdom (12:25); the strong man's house (12:29); the effect of scattering (12:30); a tree known by its fruit (12:33); and the good and evil treasure (12:35). The emphasis in 12:31 upon the Spirit is directly related to the quotation from Isaiah in 12:18–21, and the mention of the Son of Man in 12:32 repeats the phrase that was part of the concluding statement of the first incident in this section (12:8). The T-CR is informed of the negative status of the Pharisees and Jesus' criticism of them.

The Pharisees and scribes again question him in the next incident (12:38–45), this time about a sign from heaven. Jesus' response is a more direct attack, which he begins by characterizing the questioners as an "evil and adulterous generation" (12:39). For the T-CR this is important as a continuation of the definition of evil from the previous incident (12:35). The meaning of the sign of Jonah is described by comparing Jonah's three days and three nights in the fish with the Son of Man's three days and nights in the heart of the earth, another use of metaphor. It is further illustrated with the men of Nineveh and the queen of the South. The use of the term "greater" (12:41–42) is similar to the statement in 12:6 about Jesus being greater than the temple. Thus the T-CR learns of another instance of Jesus' use of metaphors and his opposition to the Pharisees.

The connections between these incidents inform the T-CR of the negative features of the Pharisees and their influence as antitypes of the disciples. At the conclusion of this section, a story of a man with unclean spirits (12:43–45), there is an example of "this evil generation" (12:45) which underlines the generations' contrast with Jesus who has received the Spirit of the Father.

Section D ends with a reaffirmation of the importance of the disciples (12:46–50) and affirms how distinct they are from the Pharisees. Jesus says his "mother" and "brothers" are the disciples; they are the ones who do "the will of my Father in heaven" (12:50). The disciples are mentioned at the conclusion of the section and thereby stand in complete contrast to Jesus' opponents. It is especially important for the T-CR that the disciples are defined here as those who do the Father's will.

Section E (Immediate Context 13:1–50): The story shifts again when the narrator reports that Jesus begins to teach a large crowd gathered by the sea. Rather than replying to questions or accusations from the Pharisees, Jesus himself initiates this portion of the story; it is the narrator's phrase that stands out: "He told them many things in parables" (13:3). Since this is the first time the word "parable" has been used in the story, its definition is formed by Jesus' words in the story of the sower (13:3–9).

When the disciples ask why he speaks to the crowd in parables (13:10), Jesus' answer helps the T-CR comprehend the term "parable" and the role of the disciples. Jesus' reply distinguishes between the disciples and others ("them") who have not received the capacity "to know the secrets of the kingdom of heaven" (13:11). This sets the context for the explanation of the story of the sower, in which there is a clear distinction between the disciples ("to you") and the crowd ("them"). Jesus makes it clear that he has a high expectation, not evaluation, of the disciples because they have been given the capacity to know; they have been chosen, they follow, and they are the ones who have more and who could receive more. One aspect of this capability is defined in 13:13, the ability to see and comprehend, to hear and understand. The value of this potential finds support in another fulfillment quotation (13:14–15), this time stated by Jesus himself, which emphasizes not only the importance of following the Father's will or purpose, but also verifies the importance of the role which the disciples are expected to play. In the final two statements (13:16–17) of his answer, Jesus clearly distinguishes the disciples from other important and positive individuals from the past; they rank above "many of the prophets and righteous men" (13:17). Thus the T-CR has been informed of the importance of the prophets and about those who are, or should be, righteous (1:19, 5:45, 9:13, 10:41 [three times], 13:17).

Since the disciples have the *capacity* to know the secrets of the kingdom, it is logical that Jesus would explain the parable of the sower (13:18–23). The climax of the explanation repeats the emphases already mentioned, that the good soil represents those who hear the word and understand it. Jesus clearly expects the disciples to comprehend the message presented through the parables, that is, in metaphors, which resembles the message conveyed earlier in the narrative, especially the goal of the followers to be "fishers of people." There is nothing unusual, then, when he continues to speak to the crowd in parables. Those who have the capacity will be able to understand. The narrative changes pace at 13:34 with the narrator's summary statement, followed once again by a fulfillment quotation stressing the close connection between the Father and Jesus' message.

The focus on the disciples intensifies in 13:36 when the disciples come to Jesus and ask for an explanation of the parable of the weeds. The T-CR is thereby influenced to question the ability of the disciples to understand; do they indeed have the capability to comprehend as Jesus expects? It would appear that they need more help. Since the narrator reports that Jesus immediately launches into an explanation of the parable, it would seem that Jesus recognizes this fact. This is especially the case when Jesus continues, after explaining the parable of the weeds, to present more parables to the disciples. The disciples' ability to comprehend the way he uses metaphors seems to be confirmed by the way he speaks to them. As a result, the T-CR is encouraged to view the disciples as qualified followers.

Thus, the context which sets the stage for this character-shaping incident, Jesus' question about whether the disciples understood "all this," has been consistent. It is no surprise to the T-CR when they reply "yes," and the positive attitude of Jesus is reinforced in the final metaphor.

Summary

The image of the disciples portrayed in incident three is positive. It indicates that they think they have reached a new level in meeting Jesus' expectations. Within the larger context for character-shaping incident three, the T-CR receives more detailed indication of Jesus' expectations: the disciples are not merely to follow but to perform miraculous deeds. Prior to this incident, there has been no indication whether they have acted as Jesus expects. However, his response to their affirmative answer indicates that he does find the answer acceptable. In addition, the continuing contrast drawn between the disciples and the Pharisees gives the T-CR a positive view of the disciples.

The limited portrait of the disciples up to this point in the story has mixed positive, anticipatory, and critical information for the T-CR. The four early followers (from the first character-shaping incident) responded to Jesus' request and promise. They were willing to follow a Jesus presented to the T-CR as a son of God in continuity with God's earlier actions and words. However, the T-CR was not informed of the reason for the followers' apparent positive reaction.

When the disciples/followers were confronted with trouble in character-shaping incident two, however, the T-CR saw that they did not meet Jesus' expectations. Jesus defined them as "men of little faith" and thus they were contrasted with two individuals who previously had been shown to have faith. Jesus had tried to inform them of his high expectations for them as disciples, and they had witnessed his ability to control certain major events, yet they were not yet able to rely on him at a time of great distress.

After the critical assessment in incident two, the disciples are not portrayed in any specific way — although one of the twelve is described by the narrator as a betrayer. However, the T-CR learns more about Jesus' expectations of the disciples and the problems that he indicates may confront them as his followers. It is obviously important to learn of Jesus' reference to his disciples as his family — defined as "whoever does the will of my father in heaven." Such a statement gives the T-CR a positive image of Jesus' current evaluation, but the T-CR does not receive any report of the disciples' response, and therefore no modification of their portrayal. The primary question for the T-CR is: How will they live up to Jesus' expectations and current evaluation?

Given this context, the T-CR gains a positive image of the disciples in incident three. Since they have been portrayed as distinct from the Pharisees and have listened to Jesus as he teaches the crowd with parables, they claim to have the ability to understand the meaning of Jesus' parables. Since they had received teaching earlier regarding Jesus' expectation of them as disciples, it is implied that they have gained enough insight to comprehend his metaphoric teaching. Jesus further defines them as having the capacity to understand him, and then, when he asks if they have comprehended his parables, they claim to have reached this expectation. Jesus does not verify if they have understood; rather, he accepts their positive response by continuing with another metaphorical teaching.

Thus, the T-CR's image of the disciples changes once again, this time positively. However, there is no clear portrayal of the disciples' capability — through action — of meeting Jesus' high expectation. The T-CR, while given reason to anticipate a growing positive attitude toward the disciples, has not as yet received clear proof with which to verify this expectation.

Character-Shaping Incident Four:

THE WALKING ON THE WATER
Matt. 14:22–33

T HE EXPANDED PORTION (13:53–14:36) of the chart for incident four demonstrates that chapter 13 ends with Jesus in dialogue. The disciples are not listed "on scene" because the narrator does not mention them as following Jesus to his own country. Chapter 14 begins with the narrator's account of Herod's response to "the fame of Jesus" (14:1) and presents a flashback (an earlier incident) about John the Baptist's death. Therefore, Jesus is also listed "off scene" when chapter 14 begins. Matthew's story continues with Jesus and the disciples returning "on scene" (14:13). After the feeding of five thousand people (14:13–21), character-shaping incident four takes place. Peter and the disciples are involved in the story about Jesus walking on the water. The disciples' response gives the T-CR a more detailed portrait of their understanding of Jesus.

Details of Event

Incident four occurring soon after incident three is a disciple character-shaping incident because it combines action, sayings, and two responses.

> [22]Then he made the disciples get into the boat and go before him to the other side, while he dismissed the crowds. [23]And after he had dismissed the crowds, he went up into the hills to pray. When evening came he was there alone, [24]but the boat by this time was many furlongs distant from the land, beaten by the waves; for the wind was against them. [25]And in the fourth watch of the night he came to them, walking on the sea. [26]But when the disciples saw him walking on the sea, they were terrified, saying, "It is a ghost!" And they cried out for fear. [27]But immediately he spoke to them, saying, "Take heart, it is I; have no fear." [28]And Peter answered him, "Lord, if it is you, bid me come to you on the water." [29]He said, "Come." So Peter got out of the boat and walked on the water and came to Jesus; [30]but when he saw the wind, he was afraid,

Disciple Character-Shaping Analysis #4: Matthew 14:22–33
Expanded Section: Matthew 13:53–14:36

DISCIPLES

On Scene

Response

INCIDENT

JESUS

To Disciples

Dialogue

Teaching

Miracles

On Scene

14

14

*

and beginning to sink he cried out, "Lord, save me." [31]Jesus immediately reached out his hand and caught him, saying to him, "O man of little faith, why did you doubt?" [32]And when they got into the boat, the wind ceased. [33]And those in the boat worshipped him, saying, "Truly you are the Son of God."

The order of action in the narrator's report is interesting. The narrator reports that Jesus "compelled" the disciples to get in the boat to precede him to the other side of the lake "while he dismissed the crowds" (14:22). As usual, the T-CR is not informed whether the disciples complied and must anticipate that this gap will be filled as the story flows forward. Then, after repeating that Jesus dismissed the crowds, the narrator reports that Jesus went up on the mountain by himself to pray (14:23). The T-CR has already been informed about the importance of prayer: In chapters 5 and 6, when Jesus is educating the disciples, they are told how to pray and its importance for being in contact with the Father.

The next phrase, "when evening came" (14:23), implies that Jesus had been alone for some time. The main clause of the sentence, however, repeats the fact of his isolation. The focus shifts back to the disciples immediately and to their situation. Their boat is far removed in the lake and beaten by the waves because the wind is against them (14:24). Thus the T-CR learns that they had obeyed Jesus' command to go by boat to the other side. Then the T-CR is told directly that late in the night Jesus came to them, walking on the sea (14:25). The T-CR is not informed of the reason for Jesus' action; the implication based on the order of the report is that he wanted to join them, having compelled them to make the journey "before him" (14:22).

The narrator then reports how the disciples respond when they see him: "They were terrified, saying, 'It is a ghost.' And they cried out for fear" (14:26). It is clear that they did not expect such an action from Jesus. It is not clear whether they know who it is; the narrator says they "saw him" but refers to the one walking on the water as a "ghost." The disciples are portrayed, therefore, up to this point as reacting to the immediate situation and are either confused about this action of Jesus or not aware that it is Jesus. The narrator reports a further reaction when it is said that they "cried out for fear" (14:26). The T-CR must fill in the reason for their fear. If they fear Jesus because he appears as a ghost, the implication would seem to be that they have not yet understood his capability to act in unusual ways.

The narrator reports, next, that Jesus immediately said, "Take heart, it is I; have no fear" (14:27). Thus the T-CR is informed about how to interpret Jesus' action — as an attempt to help the disciples and to recognize that their surprise and terror are comprehensible. The T-CR has been informed prior to this event about the meaning of the word "fear" in this narrative world. In the story's framework, the angel of the Lord told Joseph not to "fear to take Mary as your wife" (1:20), indicating that not fearing is understanding a specific event as a result of the Father's action. Therefore, fear is a failure to recognize the deeper meaning of a certain event. Joseph is also afraid (2:22) to go back to Judea when returning from Egypt. His fear is appropriate, the narrator indicates, by reporting that he is later warned in a dream to do just as he had thought he should. Thus the word "fear," at this point, is directly related to one's non-recognition of God's actions and requirements. The T-CR has also been informed that the crowd which witnesses Jesus' healing of the paralytic was "afraid, and they glorified God, who had given such authority to men" (9:8).

Thus, before the speech to the apostles (10:5–42) the T-CR has received different understandings of the word "fear." However, in the second speech to the apostles, "fear" is used four times in the section in which Jesus emphasizes the positive connection between the disciple and his teacher (10:24–33). The disciples are told not to fear those who malign a master's householders because such an action, and apparently its intent, is known by the Father. But they are then told that they *should* fear the one who "can destroy both soul and body in hell" (10:28); he is the source of life and death (10:26–28). They should *not* have fear because of *their* value: "You are of more value than many sparrows" (10:31). This section ends by rephrasing the beginning of the section: if you act as one of my servants or householders, I will act in your behalf with the Father. If you deny me, and are not acting as a disciple should act, you will be denied before the Father. The word "fear" was also used to describe the reason for Herod's decision to behead John the Baptist — he was afraid of the people who would be critical if he executed someone they considered a prophet (14:5). Herod is portrayed as someone more concerned about how his people respond than about the Father's requirements. In this narrative world, fear is good or bad depending on its relation to the Father. Thus, in this incident the word "fear," for the T-CR, indicates that the disciples do not understand the Father's will and action.

The primary meaning, for the T-CR, of Jesus' response to the disciples' fear is that Jesus identifies himself and thereby contrasts himself to their description of him as a "ghost." He recognizes their problem and understands that they do not accept him as the Father's son.

The reaction of the disciples to Jesus' identification and request is clear when the narrator reports that one of the disciples, Peter, speaks out. Peter is known by the T-CR as the first disciple in the list of the twelve in 10:2, the first of the four fishermen (4:18), and the person whose mother-in-law was healed by Jesus (8:14). He is obviously associated with the group of disciples and has been focused on, as an individual, more than any other member of that group up to this point. The T-CR is guided to see Peter as an active member of the group of twelve.

Peter's request to walk on the water (14:28) implies that he recognizes Jesus' sonship: He uses the title "Lord" followed by the conditional, "If it is you." Since Jesus did not use his own name but expected the disciples to recognize him, Peter indicates that he does draw the connection and has some confidence in Jesus' power over the natural world when he says, "Bid me come to you on the water" (14:28). Jesus' response is precise: "Come." The T-CR is thereby informed that Jesus accepts Peter's request as possible; it is not outrageous. Peter is portrayed as knowing that Jesus could enable him to walk on the water — he expresses his respect for Jesus' authority, as one in close relation to the Father.

The narrator reports a continuation of the miracle, in effect, when he says that Peter did walk on the water to come to Jesus. Thus, Peter is able to do what he and Jesus wanted. But after reporting that Peter sees the wind and reporting his negative reaction to it ("he was afraid"), the narrator says that Peter begins to sink into the lake and has to ask for help, "Lord, save me." This is a second request, this time desperate and similar to the disciples' request for rescue from their sinking boat in character-shaping incident two (8:25). The narrator states the reason for Peter's fear and need for help: "When he saw the wind, he was afraid" (14:30). The T-CR is led to bring incident two into the foreground. As in 8:22–27, the wind is the source of the problem; although Jesus can control it, it is a source of trouble and danger. Thus the environment again creates fear in a disciple, even though the T-CR has seen previously the disciples' significant progress in their attempt to comprehend Jesus. Peter seems to have confidence in Jesus; he knows what Jesus can do, and yet he is negatively influenced by the presence of the wind.

The word "wind" occurs three times prior to this incident, all of which inform the T-CR that it is a negative force which (1) endangers the houses in the parable at the end of the first teaching of the disciples (7:25, 27), (2) endangers the disciples and Jesus in the boat in incident two (8:26–27), and (3) disturbs the reed in Jesus' metaphoric description of John the Baptist (11:7). In *this* incident, as in incident two, the wind causes Peter to fear; that is, he interprets it as an occurrence which does not represent the action of the Father. The wind is seen as a problem for walking on the sea.

The narrator then reports that Jesus "immediately reached out his hand and caught him, saying to him, 'O man of little faith, why did you doubt?'" (14:31). This response is the crux for understanding Peter. It is clear that Jesus expected a more positive or stable response from Peter.

He labels Peter with a phrase used earlier, "person of little faith." The T-CR was informed previously (1) that those who are *anxious* about clothing or food (6:30) are designated as having little faith; and (2) that the men in the boat who wake Jesus (8:26), because they are worried about their safety, are addressed as those of "little faith." Thus having little faith is a clear criticism for the T-CR. Jesus expects followers to comprehend his close relation to the Father. However, in this incident the word "doubt" is used, for the first time in this narrative world, as an equivalent to fear; the narrator describes Peter's problem as fear, but Jesus refers to it as "doubt." Given this limited information, to be of little faith is to doubt or fear, which, given the earlier uses of "fear," is for the T-CR a failure to see how one is in the Father's hands.

Peter, therefore, is criticized by Jesus because he should not have been affected by the supposed threat perceived in the wind. That he begins to sink demonstrates that his "faith" has deteriorated and that Jesus is able to help him, that is, save him. The significance of the wind is emphasized in the next sentence: "And when they got into the boat, the wind ceased" (14:32). Although Jesus is not reported to have rebuked the wind, as he did in incident two (8:22–27), the similarity to that incident is significant for the T-CR.

The final statement in this incident is from the narrator who reports that the disciples worshipped Jesus, saying, "Truly you are the son of God" (14:33). The word "worship" or "falling on one's knees" has been used previously (2:2, 8, 11; 4:9, 10; 8:2; 9:18) to indicate that the person(s) being described has, or should have, great respect for someone. For the T-CR, the meaning of "worshipped" in this incident is clarified by the quoted statement: the disciples perceive him to be "the son of God." The T-CR has been informed of this in detail and now is shown that the disciples have reached this level of understanding. This portrayal of the disciples is consistent with the previous character-shaping incident in that the information is positive. The disciples' claim to have understood the parables of the kingdom is now manifest in their comprehension of this event, even though Peter is unable to perform perfectly. Peter demonstrates *some* faith by walking on the water, but when he begins to sink he also demonstrates his limitations. As a person of little faith, doubt, or lack of certainty, he is nonetheless part of a group that recognizes what was presented to the T-CR in the framework: Jesus is the son of God with the accompanying power and authority of the Father, especially over the wind and sea.

Thus, incident four presents the T-CR with a limited, positive view of the disciples. Once they are informed that Jesus is the "ghost" walking on the water, one of the disciples asks to participate in this action that comes from the Father. Being able to walk on the sea demonstrates a proper attitude, but after a few steps Peter must be saved by the Father's son. Finally, the disciples perceive Jesus as the son when he and Peter enter the boat.

Context

Incident four follows closely after incident three. Emphasis on the opposition to Jesus is still a primary feature.

After the positive portrayal of the disciples in incident three (13:52), when Jesus implies that he accepts the disciples' claim to understand the parables, the narrator reports that Jesus goes to his own country and teaches in the synagogue of his hometown. Described as "astonished" (13:52), the local people are quoted: "Where did this man get this wisdom and these mighty works? Is not this the carpenter's son? Is not his mother called Mary? And are not his brothers James and Joseph and Simon and Judas? And are not all his sisters with us? Where then did this man get all this?" (13:54–56). Since the T-CR already has received the word "astonished," the questions can be interpreted as skeptical and negative. This is confirmed by the narrator's conclusion: "And they took offense at him" (13:57). The contrast with the disciples is distinct. Although these people from his own country are not followers, they might be expected to respect Jesus' power and authority. Since the narrator does not report what Jesus taught them, the T-CR has to fill in the gap. The local people's focus on the family implies that they raise the questions because they are not willing to accept Jesus' close connection with the Father. His "wisdom" and "mighty works" do not carry enough weight to overcome their awareness of his family connections.

Jesus' answer (13:57) focuses on the word "prophet" and uses a metaphor: "A prophet is not without honor except in his own country and in his own house." Prophets have been identified previously as those who have spoken God's word in the past. It is especially important in the fulfillment quotations which show the close relationship between certain current events and God's earlier prophetic messages. Thus Jesus is saying that the audience's failure to recognize his relation to the Father is not unusual.

Therefore, the context for incident four begins by emphasizing that the opposition to Jesus comes from many sources — not only from the Pharisees, but also from people of his own country. The narrator's summary statement implies that Jesus withholds some of his power because of their nonfaith/unbelief (*apistian*), a word not used previously. Since "faith" has been used to show how characters identify the correct status of Jesus, the disciples, previously referred to as those with little faith, are, for the T-CR, in a small way more positive than these hometown people.

The narrator then shifts attention to Herod, the tetrarch, by quoting his statement about Jesus, "This is John the Baptist, he has been raised from the dead; that is why these powers are at work in him" (14:2). A number of things inform the T-CR. The most important is the mention of the death of John the Baptist, which the narrative has not reported until this moment, but also the problem of the reliability and rationale of Herod's statement. The narrator settles this problem immediately with a flashback validating Herod's statement about John's death and, in addition, demonstrating certain features of Herod's character. Herod was reluctant to kill John because he feared the people who considered John a prophet. John *is* executed, however, because Herod does not wish to violate the oaths he made in the presence of "the company" (14:6). The narrator says, "And the king was sorry; but because of his oaths and his guests he commanded it to be given" (14:9).

The flashback, then, not only explains the circumstances that led to John's death, but helps especially to comprehend Herod's statement about Jesus in 14:2. Herod is heavily influenced by circumstances. Since Herod had been more heavily influenced by his colleagues than the people, it means that he probably would not be reluctant to attack John again in his resurrected form, i.e., Jesus. Thus, the T-CR receives even more details about the growing number of Jesus' opponents.

Immediate Context

The flashback about John's death ends with an interesting ambiguity. The narrator reports: "Now when Jesus heard, he withdrew..." (14:13). The narrator does not indicate exactly what Jesus heard. The conclusion of the previous sentence, "[John's disciples] went and told Jesus" (14:12), based on the flow of the narrative, is part of the flashback — that John's disciples told Jesus about John's death. Therefore, what Jesus heard, as mentioned in 14:13, is Herod's statement: "This is John the Baptist, he has been raised from the dead; that is why these powers are at work in him" (14:2). Thus, the T-CR is informed that Jesus withdraws from the area after learning about Herod's understanding of Jesus, as someone who has been destroyed and should be repersecuted.

The disciples are again directly involved in the next incident, the feeding of the five thousand. The narrator explicitly states Jesus' attitude toward the crowd: "He had compassion on them" (14:14). When the miracle is initiated, by the disciples' concern about the hunger of the crowd (14:15), they are told to feed them. The disciples reply that they do not have enough food, and therefore Jesus blesses the five loaves and two fish and gives them to the disciples to distribute. This provides a positive view of the disciples to the T-CR; they have concern for the crowd and willingly assist Jesus. Their reaction to the miraculous feeding, or the response of anyone else, is not reported. Thus the T-CR is left with a gap about its impact upon the disciples.

Summary

After incident three the T-CR has been guided toward a positive image of the disciples. Knowing that the disciples need to be trained or educated to become fishers of people, and having witnessed two sizable sections of the story in which Jesus teaches them of his expectations and concerns, the T-CR has a clear idea in what direction they should be moving. Following their earlier claim to have understood Jesus' teaching in metaphorical stories, and Jesus' apparent acceptance of their ability to understand (in character-shaping incident three), the disciples are portrayed in this incident as having improved in their recognition of Jesus.

The context for this incident informed the T-CR that the disciples are distinctly *different* from the people in Jesus' own country. Although the people of his home country are not as aggressive as the Pharisees, they are portrayed as opposed to Jesus despite his status as a prophet.

The growing opposition to Jesus receives further emphasis in the story of John the Baptist's death. Herod's execution of John is likely to be the kind of action taken by those critical of Jesus. John was presented as someone close to the Father, but is nevertheless killed by a political leader. Thus for the T-CR the kind of problems that the disciples may expect is underlined. However, the disciples have not abandoned Jesus — they follow him and help in distributing his gifts to the hungry people.

Thus, the T-CR is given a negative view of disciples when Peter is criticized because of his fear and doubt, though he had enough understanding both to ask to walk on the water with Jesus and to do it. He is still a man of *little* faith.

Nevertheless, with the disciples' explicit statement that they recognize Jesus as a son of God, the T-CR is given a very *positive* characterization. The narrator has clearly informed the T-CR of one of the main features of the framework in this narrative world: Jesus is indeed to be understood as the son of the Father. Just as incident three made it look like the disciples had taken a step forward, though they were not precisely shown to have improved, incident four also has negative and positive elements in its portrayal. The T-CR is informed of Peter's limited capability and, at the conclusion, is informed of a positive response showing that the disciples are moving toward the recognition of the reality of

Jesus as the son of the Father—something the T-CR has been informed about from the beginning.

The disciples have therefore been portrayed as having *some* faith. The T-CR has been shown that they have progressed in the right direction.

Character-Shaping Incident Five:

THE CAESAREA PHILIPPI
INTERACTION
Matt. 16:5–23

A S THE CHART for this incident displays, the interaction between Jesus and his disciples has increased significantly in the central portion of Matthew's story. The context for this event, the development of the story between character-shaping incidents four and five, consists primarily of Jesus in dialogue. The response of the disciples moves in a steady pattern and, although this character-shaping incident (16:5–23) is one of a series of responses in this section of the Gospel, it is considered character-shaping because it reveals specific information about the disciples' capability to be true followers.

Details of Event

This incident forms a relatively lengthy portion of the narrative. After an indication that the disciples could understand Jesus' metaphor of the leaven, Peter signals their recognition of Jesus as the son of the Father. However, Peter is unable to accept Jesus' statement of his suffering, death, and resurrection as an appropriate fate. When read in sequence, the impact on the T-CR's evaluation of the disciples is indeed significant.

> [5]When the disciples reached the other side, they had forgotten to bring any bread. [6]Jesus said to them, "Take heed and beware of the leaven of the Pharisees and Sadducees." [7]And they discussed it among themselves, saying, "We brought no bread." [8]But Jesus, aware of this, said, "O men of little faith, why do you discuss among yourselves the fact that you have no bread? [9]Do you not yet perceive? Do you not remember the five loaves of the five thousand, and how many baskets you gathered? [10]Or the seven loaves of the four thousand, and how many baskets you gathered? [11]How is it that you fail to perceive that I did not speak about bread? Beware of the leaven of the Pharisees and Sadducees." [12]Then they

*Disciple Character-Shaping Analysis #5: Matthew 16:5–23
Expanded Section: Matthew 14:34–17:1*

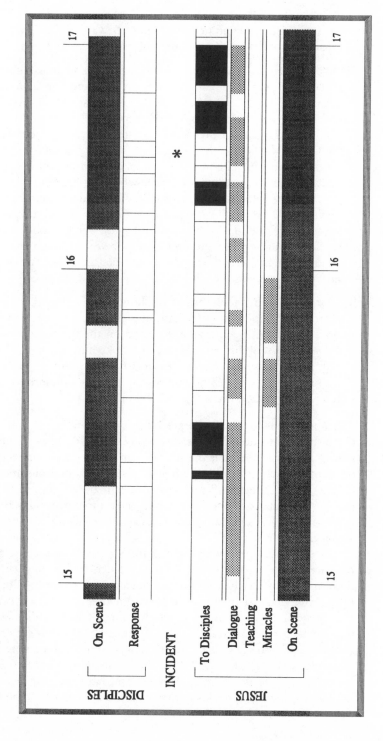

understood that he did not tell them to beware of the leaven of the bread, but of the teaching of the Pharisees and Sadducees.

[13]Now when Jesus came into the district of Caesarea Philippi, he asked his disciples, "Who do men say that the Son of Man is?" [14]And they said, "Some say John the Baptist, others say Elijah, and others Jeremiah or one of the prophets." [15]He said to them, "But who do you say that I am?" [16]Simon Peter replied, "You are the Christ, the Son of the living God." [17]And Jesus answered him, "Blessed are you, Simon Bar-Jonah! For flesh and blood has not revealed this to you, but my father who is in heaven. [18]And I tell you, you are Peter, and on this rock I will build my church, and the powers of death shall not prevail against it. [19]I will give you the keys of the kingdom of heaven, and whatever you bind on earth shall be bound in heaven, and whatever you loose on earth shall be loosed in heaven." [20]Then he strictly charged the disciples to tell no one that he was the Christ.

[21]From that time Jesus began to show his disciples that he must go to Jerusalem and suffer many things from the elders and chief priests and scribes, and be killed, and on the third day be raised. [22]And Peter took him and began to rebuke him, saying, "God forbid, Lord! This shall never happen to you." [23]But he turned and said to Peter, "Get behind me, Satan! You are a hindrance to me; for you are not on the side of God, but of men."

There are a series of characterization statements in this incident: the disciples are described as discussing with one another after Jesus speaks to them (16:5–7); the narrator presents an omniscient description of the disciples' understanding of Jesus' five questions and warning (16:12); Jesus replies to Peter's answer to the question of Jesus' identity (16:17–19); Peter responds as a spokesperson for the group (16:16–19); Peter rebukes Jesus (16:22); and Jesus replies critically to Peter's second statement (16:23).

The sequence begins with the narrator's report that the disciples "had forgotten to bring any bread" (16:5). Since the feeding of the four thousand was described just a few verses earlier (15:32–39), the narrator's reference to bread does not seem out of place: it brings into the foreground the feeding miracle for the T-CR and also sets a context for this incident. Jesus' initial statement (16:6), an exhortation of caution about the leaven of the Pharisees and Sadducees, is therefore particularly relevant for the T-CR. The Pharisees and Sadducees are portrayed as opponents of Jesus (16:1–4) and had just been put down by him. Thus, the metaphoric character of Jesus' saying is emphasized for the T-CR.

The narrator next reports the disciples' reaction, with the preliminary comment that they discussed it among themselves, implying that they did not recognize the metaphorical meaning of Jesus' exhortation (16:7). The quotation from the disciples' discussion indicates that they interpret the warning literally: "We brought no bread." Since the narrator began the incident by reporting that they had indeed forgotten to bring bread, that the statement is a literal misinterpretation is quite clear. The disciples are thereby presented to the T-CR as dull or unimaginative, especially in light of their earlier claim to have understood the parables.

Jesus' next response (16:8–11), showing he knows of their discussion, indicates that the disciples have done more than merely misunderstand; he again uses the phrase "men of little faith," thereby clarifying for the T-CR the importance, for Jesus, of their lack of comprehension. That Jesus' lengthy response consists of five rhetorical questions followed by a repetition of the original warning about the leaven of the Pharisees and Sadducees conveys to the T-CR a sense of Jesus' frustration based on their inability to perceive. In effect, the narrator has brought to the foreground for the T-CR (1) the disciples' claim that they did understand the parables in chapter 13, (2) the importance of the first feeding miracle in chapter 14 (vv. 13–21), and (3) the second feeding in chapter 15 (vv. 32–39). The last rhetorical question that affirms Jesus' earlier warning was based on a metaphorical comparison: "How is it that you fail to perceive that I did not speak about bread?" (16:11).

Jesus' expectation becomes clear to the T-CR with the repetition of the verb "perceive" (16:9, 11). Jesus had used the word once before (15:17) when asking the disciples if they had again misunderstood a metaphorical statement. In 16:9 the word is again part of a rhetorical question, "Do you not yet perceive...," which implies that the disciples might perceive in the future. In 16:11, however, although the word is still in a question, it is not a question that asks whether the disciples *will* perceive but *why* they *did not* perceive or understand. The T-CR is informed that the disciples are criticized because of their inability to comprehend Jesus' use of metaphors and parables. Thus, the T-CR is informed of the disciples' inability to reach Jesus' expectations.

After Jesus' forthright criticism of the disciples, the narrator's conclusion (16:12) is doubly important. The T-CR, who has, up to this point, received both positive and negative information about the disciples, is now informed by the narrator that, when confronted by Jesus' rhetorical questions, they are able to grasp his meaning. Rather than reporting the disciples' words or action, the narrator acts omnisciently by showing that they understand that the leaven refers to the teaching of the Pharisees and Sadducees. This omniscient description has immediate impact on the T-CR with regard to the status of the disciples as those who do perceive (as in chapter 13), although it takes a bit of specific questioning. The description also makes certain that the T-CR comprehends the message. Omniscient description is not used very often in this narrative and stands out as the affirmation of the narrator, whose reliability for the T-CR is as positive as that of Jesus. Thus the negative portrait of the disciples present at the beginning of the incident turns around. The disciples have been presented as a dull and slow group, but, when prodded in the right direction and confronted with the possibility that there is a deeper meaning than they had at first recognized, they are portrayed as educable, capable of finally realizing the importance of the metaphorical dimension of Jesus' message.

The next part (16:13–21) of this incident flows smoothly from the preceding action. The subordinate clause beginning the sentence makes the change of location of lesser importance and moves the emphasis to the main clause: "He asked his disciples, 'Who do men say that the Son of Man is?' " The T-CR has been informed about the phrase "Son of Man" in seven previous incidents. It was a phrase used only by Jesus about himself when he was speaking to the scribes, Pharisees, crowd, and disciples. For example, in Jesus' explanation to the disciples of the parable of the weeds of the field, the sower of the good seed is the "Son of Man" (13:37). Although this title is never directly explained, the context has been consistent enough to inform the T-CR that Jesus is referring to himself in incident five — and, if the disciples understand his metaphors, the meaning will be clear to them. Thus the T-CR's attention continues to be focused on the disciples.

Their response to this question, which asks what others have said about the Son of Man's identity, is also informative. That some who have followed and listened would not have a full understanding of Jesus is consistent with the information already supplied to the T-CR. But, when Jesus immediately asks the same question of the disciples (16:15), the focus continues on the disciples and their understanding of him. It is also clear that the reference to the Son of Man in the previous question was a reference to himself.

Peter's reply ("You are the Christ, the Son of the living God") demonstrates how far the disciples have come. There can be little doubt that Peter is portrayed as a spokesperson for the group because Jesus' question was addressed to "them." They realize that Jesus is the anointed one who fulfills the Father's will and that he is indeed the son of the Father, repeating their previously stated understanding of Jesus after he had walked on the water (14:33). This information about Jesus has been presented consistently to the T-CR in previous narrative and thus, for the T-CR, Peter's reply is accurate. Jesus also suggests the accuracy of Peter's answer by first declaring Peter "blessed," a characteristic of those honored by the Father as Jesus had stated in his first teaching of the disciples (5:3–11). In a limited way the disciples have acted as Jesus has expected. However, Jesus immediately qualifies his acknowledgment of the truth of Peter's statement by saying that this accurate understanding of his status comes from the Father and not from Peter himself. The impact on the T-CR of this statement about how Peter has been influenced and guided cannot be overstressed. Jesus, the Father's Son, who has just congratulated Peter on his achievement, ascribes it to the influence of the Father.

At this point the T-CR learns that Jesus' attempt to mold his twelve followers has made significant progress and that the rest of the narrative will describe their combined, parallel movement toward the goal of Jesus' mission. The disciples are thus portrayed as distinct from the crowd and distant from the Pharisees and Sadducees.

This point is emphasized in the remainder of the short, positive response from Jesus. Using another metaphor, he focuses on Peter's name; he continues to honor Peter by declaring him the foundation for his community which will stand up to the force of Satan. Second, by shifting the metaphorical image to a doorway, Jesus declares Peter to be the holder of the keys of the kingdom, with the power to bind and release because of his openness to the message from the Father. Such a positive response to a disciple from Jesus is certainly unusual for the T-CR and dramatically underscores the importance and accuracy of Peter's statement. Peter is not portrayed, then, as an ideal individual but as a follower who is open to the influence and wisdom of the Father.

Thus the T-CR's information about the disciples has increased. Jesus' expectation has been partially fulfilled by his recognition that Peter is a follower guided by the Father — someone who is open to such influence.

The narrator continues by reporting that Jesus "strictly charged the disciples" (not just Peter) "to tell no one that he was the Christ" (16:20). The command seems to reverse the tone of the incident. By requiring the disciples to contain within their group the insight that the Father gives them, Jesus is shown to understand the Father's purpose in having revealed Jesus' status to Peter — to make certain that the disciples are fully informed about Jesus' status but also to withhold this information from other people in the story.

In the final section of the incident, the disciples are again the focus when the narrator does not quote Jesus but merely summarizes his teaching about the requirement that he must go to Jerusalem, suffer, be killed, and be raised (16:21). For the first time, the T-CR has been informed that Jesus understands the negative response to his teaching about the coming of the kingdom.

Peter's response (16:22), which the narrator describes as rebuking, is preceded by the report that Peter "took him aside"; that is, the conversation between Jesus and Peter is in private. The rebuke itself reflects Peter's understanding of Jesus' importance: "(Father be) merciful *to you,*

Lord! This will never be [or happen] *to you*." Peter's response, therefore, challenges Jesus' prediction, as reported by the narrator. In its swearing, explanatory content, it is an immediate and intense response. In effect, Peter says that *he* understands the Father's wishes as contrary to the son's prediction: the Father will never allow this to happen to you. The narrator calls Peter's reply a "rebuke" *before* it is quoted, thereby showing the T-CR how it should be judged.

Jesus' response (16:23) to Peter's rebuke is direct: the disciple praised for being guided by the Father is *now criticized* for being influenced by Satan. In reply to both of Peter's responses in this incident, Jesus states that Peter is not speaking on his own. Peter speaks first as a spokesperson for the Father and, second, for Satan. The T-CR is thereby informed that when Jesus attempts to teach the disciples details about his true character — what it means for him to be the son of the Father — the disciples, on their own, cannot recognize the teachings' validity. A disciple is portrayed as one who can be influenced by either the Father or Satan. The second part of Jesus' response helps the T-CR comprehend his reaction by, in effect, defining the Satan-like character of the statement. Peter is declared to be a stumbling block, as opposed to a foundation rock, because he does not think the things of the Father but the things of people. Thereby Satan and people are identified as opposed to the Father.

The T-CR has been clearly informed about Satan. It is a word used by Jesus in two previous incidents: when he speaks (4:10) to the tempter, whom the narrator refers to as the devil (4:1, 5, 8, 11); and when he responds to the Pharisees' statement that he casts out demons by the prince of demons, arguing the illogical assumption that Satan casts out Satan (12:26). Thus there is a direct correlation among demons who are cast out, unclean spirits, Satan, and the devil. The interconnection of these terms is clearly presented to the T-CR in the temptation story, in Jesus' first teaching of the disciples, in casting-out miracles, in dialogue with opponents, and in an explanation of a parable.

As a result, the T-CR can attach to Peter not only openness to positive or negative supernatural influences, but also an inability or unwillingness to recognize the source of this influence. A proper disciple, Jesus indicates, is one capable of judging the source of the influence that comes upon him.

Context

To better understand the way the T-CR is influenced by this incident we must look at the five incidents between character-shaping incident four (14:22–33) and this incident (16:5–23). Although the disciples are not present for some of these events, the relation between the events indicates that their presence is implied.

A. The first context section is a narrator's summary (14:34–36). After the positive response of the disciples to the calming of the storm in incident four the narrator reports that Jesus travels to Gennesaret (14:34). Jesus' authority and power continue to be stressed in a general report about his healing (14:35–36). The narrator emphasizes that the residents of that region, upon recognizing him, brought to Jesus those who were sick. These folk were healed merely by touching the fringe of his garment, a healing that parallels the healing of the woman with the hemorrhage in 9:22. She was healed, it was stated, because she had great faith. The same implication is presented here to the T-CR, in addition to the fact that the disciples witness both events and should therefore be aware of the basis for the healings. The narrator implies that the disciples accompany Jesus when he says "they" at the start of the report (14:34).

B. In the second context incident, the narrator emphasizes the importance of the location of these healings, Gennesaret, by reporting that the Pharisees and scribes came to Jesus from Jerusalem (15:1). Since the narrator does not mention the reason for their journey, the T-CR must refer to the previous reference (12:14) in which the Pharisees are reported to be seeking to destroy Jesus. Since the antagonism of the Pharisees has been clearly presented, the T-CR would be affected when they accuse the disciples of not washing their hands when they eat. This incident indicates that, in the minds of the Pharisees, there is a close relationship between Jesus and the disciples. In order to attack Jesus they accuse the disciples of "transgressing the tradition of the elders" (15:2).

Rather than answering directly, Jesus turns the emphasis from the disciples by first asking the Pharisees and scribes why they themselves transgress the commandment of God "for the sake of your tradition" (15:3). Jesus' explanation for asking such a question begins with two quotes, stated as God's commandments: "Honor your father and your mother" and "He who speaks evil of father or mother, let him surely die" (15:4). The quotes are followed by the phrase "but you say" (15:5), which is similar to the phrase he used in his first teaching about his support of the law and prophets (5:20–45). The emphasis then was on how his requirements go to the root of the demands of the Father. In this incident he quotes the Pharisees to demonstrate how they avoid the basic intent of the requirement, rather than seeking its radical emphasis. They are accused of making "void the word of God" by finding a way to "not honor" their father (15:6). Thus, with the debate taking place in Gennesaret, the T-CR is being informed that its people, who have recognized Jesus as a healer, apparently follow his requirements and are thereby much closer to the demands of the Father than the Pharisees.

Having given a specific example of the Pharisees' and scribes' trans-

gression of the commandment of God, Jesus refers to them as "hypocrites" and quotes Isaiah to support his criticism (15:7–9). Hypocrites
have been clearly defined for the T-CR. In his first teaching of the disciples, Jesus used the term "hypocrite" to label those whose "piety" is
the opposite of what is expected of the disciples. Hypocrites give alms,
pray, and fast so that they may be seen by people (6:1–18), and they do
not recognize their own limitations (7:5). Jesus emphasizes that the disciples should act to fulfill the Father's requirements, not to please other
humans.

There is no indication of any response by the disciples, or by the
people, to Jesus' question and criticism. Thus the T-CR receives more
information about Jesus' criticism of those contrasted with the disciples.

After Jesus' response to the question of the Pharisees, the narrator
reports that Jesus calls the people and begins to speak to them (15:10);
the Pharisees and disciples are still on scene. The message begins with a
command: hear and understand. Jesus then expands the meaning of his
response with a proverb-like statement, saying that a human is defiled
by what comes out of one's mouth, not by what goes into it (15:10).
Thus, the T-CR is informed that Jesus again speaks to the people in
metaphor — a consistent element in Jesus' teaching and something the
disciples claim to understand.

The disciples respond, reports the narrator, by coming and asking
whether Jesus realizes that he has offended the Pharisees (15:12). The
T-CR is not informed about whether the disciples indeed comprehended
the statement, but knows that the disciples are concerned about the attitude of the Pharisees. Whether the Pharisees themselves understood
the statement is also not stated. Jesus' reply (15:13–14) to the disciples' question begins indirectly with a metaphor about plants that
will be uprooted if *not* planted by his Father. Jesus then directly advises the disciples to let the Pharisees alone, for they are blind guides
(15:14). The T-CR has thus been clearly informed about the meaning
of the metaphor. What the Pharisees say is unacceptable to Jesus and
what they recommend is clearly opposed to Jesus' heavenly Father. The
proper interpretation is indicated by the order of the sentences and the
progression of the imagery, from plants to blindness.

It is a surprise, then, when the disciples respond with a request from
Peter ("Explain the parable to us"), since the disciples had said earlier
(13:52) that they understood such metaphors. Jesus' response is important: He asks if Peter is still "without understanding" (15:16). This
word, "understanding," was not used in the story previously, but the
T-CR receives a parallel term in the following question: "Do you not
perceive?" (15:17). Thus two terms designate what Jesus requires of
those who hear a parable or other metaphoric statements. The disciples are expected to comprehend Jesus' teaching — as has been clearly

stated previously. This expectation helps set the context for the T-CR for incident five (16:5–23), in which the disciples are asked about their understanding of Jesus.

The imagery Jesus uses in response to Peter's request for an explanation adds detailed information to Jesus' expectation of the disciples, who had been very specifically contrasted with the Pharisees (12:29–32, 46–50). The images of the mouth, stomach, and heart, used with relation to the source of defilement (15:17–20), focus on what Jesus considers a true follower/disciple. The T-CR receives information requiring an adjustment of the disciples' positive image, which has been developing since their response of understanding. Information is also added about Jesus' expectations and the disciples' insufficiency. As a result, it is clear that Jesus believes that the disciples have not achieved the understanding claimed in 13:52 and that he will have to continue their education. The T-CR sees that Jesus perceives the disciples to be well below the status implied earlier, but as distinct from the Pharisees.

C. The narrator initiates the third context incident (15:21–28) by reporting that Jesus "withdrew" to the district of Tyre and Sidon. It is an extended dialogue involving Jesus, the disciples, and a Canaanite woman. She requests mercy because her daughter is possessed by a demon. For the T-CR to be told of a person addressing Jesus as "Lord, son of David" is indeed unusual. At the beginning of Matthew's story, in the framework, the narrator refers to Jesus as the son of David, and an angel addresses Joseph as the son of David. No character in the narrative world has ever used this title. Thus the T-CR receives positive information about the Canaanite woman's understanding of Jesus.

However, because Jesus ignores her, the disciples say that he should send her away. Jesus appears to agree with them: "I was sent only to the lost sheep of the house of Israel" (15:24). He again replies to the disciples in a metaphor, "the lost sheep of the house of Israel." The Canaanite woman, however, makes a second request which is short and to the point: "Lord, help me" (15:25). Jesus replies with another metaphor about bread thrown to the dogs. Her response reflects a clear understanding of the metaphor. She recognizes its point and provides a good reason that he heal her daughter (15:27). Jesus' final response is similar to his response to the centurion: it is her faith which is demonstrated. The narrator reports that the exorcism occurs immediately.

The disciples, as witnesses, receive further information about Jesus' expectations, which again amount to a criticism of their request that the woman be sent away. Jesus reacts positively to the woman's statement about the dogs eating the fallen crumbs (15:27); it demonstrates to the T-CR that Jesus is open to the requests of individuals and is willing to recognize their insight if it matches that of the Father.

As indicated above, the word "faith" has been used in Matthew's story in conjunction with Jesus' healings. Its presence within individuals leads to the healing but does not actually cause it. Jesus experiences the faith of individuals when he is recognized as a healer, for example, by the centurion (8:10), by the people who bring the paralytic (9:2), by the woman with a hemorrhage (9:22), and by the blind men (9:29). Thus, this Canaanite woman displays the same respect for Jesus — the Lord and son of David — whom she is convinced can heal. She also clearly understands the metaphor which enables her to respond in a way that verifies her evaluation of Jesus.

The disciples, who, in contrast to this Canaanite woman have three times been called those of "little faith" (6:30; 8:26; 14:31), have given the T-CR more information about the meaning of faith. They are limited individuals when they (1) are anxious (6:30), (2) are concerned about their safety on a boat (8:26), and (3) are unable to continue walking on the sea, which Peter cannot do because of his fear of the wind (14:31). The T-CR has also been shown that faith is an understanding that Jesus can do the work of God, the Father (8:10, 13; 9:2, 22, 28–29).

The faith of the Canaanite woman, as presented in the limited material from this incident, is persistence and recognition that the Father is merciful to those who recognize his power, and to those who realize that Jesus is the source of that assistance. Although the narrator does not here define "faith" directly, the T-CR is informed of its importance through Jesus' positive reaction to her statement. What is learned about faith is consistent with previous information.

D. In the fourth context incident (15:29–39), the narrator begins by reporting that Jesus passed along the sea of Galilee (15:29) where crowds came to him, bringing ill people with them, whom Jesus healed (15:30). As a result, says the narrator, they "wondered [or marveled]," a term not explained in this incident except in the final statement: " . . . and they glorified the God of Israel" (15:31). The narrator has used this description previously to refer to disciples or to the crowd after Jesus performs a miracle (8:27; 9:33), and once to describe Jesus' reaction to the statement of the centurion (8:10), which Jesus called evidence of the centurion's faith. Thus the T-CR is informed that there are people of Jesus' own race who respond to him as the Canaanite woman responded. Although the disciples' presence is not mentioned, the T-CR is led to accept that they have accompanied Jesus because of their presence in the previous and the next incident. The wording in 15:30 describing the ill (lame, maimed, blind, dumb) is similar to the statement in 11:4–6 about help given to the blind, lepers, the deaf, the dead, and the poor, when Jesus answers the disciples of John the Baptist about whether he is the one to come. Thus for the T-CR this passage repeats the answer to John's question about Jesus' status and authority. In addition, the reference to the glorification of the God of Israel informs the T-CR that this event relates to the incident with the Canaanite woman: Jesus is indeed active among the lost sheep of the house of Israel. The narrator lets the T-CR know that the crowd, the direct witnesses of these healings, recognizes Jesus as one who represents the will of the Father.

The incident continues (15:32) with the report that Jesus calls the disciples and states his compassion for the hungry crowd. The disciples ask where they can get the bread to feed such a great crowd and then reply to Jesus' request about what is available. After Jesus gives thanks and breaks the food, the disciples distribute it. Since they are not mentioned again in this incident, the narrator reports no response to the feeding miracle. In addition, the narrator does not report that they accompany Jesus, who departs by boat to the region of Magadan. Despite the combined image of feeding, of food, and of giving help to people in need, the narrator does not report reactions to the event. However, since the T-CR already knows about the significance of such events, its importance as an action by the son on behalf of his Father is clear.

Immediate Context

The final context incident (16:1–4), which immediately precedes character-shaping incident five, reports that the Pharisees and Sadducees come to test Jesus by asking for a sign from heaven. Because the disciples are not mentioned as present the narrator does not focus on them. This request ("to show them a sign from heaven") is similar to the request in 12:38, asked by scribes and Pharisees. The sign of Jonah, as explained in chapter 12, is a metaphorical comparison between Jonah's days in the fish and the Son of Man's days in the heart of the earth, apparently a reference to a future event which gives the T-CR something to anticipate. Jesus' response is again metaphorical: he refers to the color of the sky and tells the Pharisees and Sadducees that they know how to interpret the sky but do not know how to interpret the signs of the times. Use of the phrase "an evil and adulterous generation" (16:4) to describe them adds more negative elements to their characterization. The emphasis on Jesus' ability to heal and perform with authority demonstrates for the T-CR the need to recognize the source of his authority. In addition, the continuing portrait of the Pharisees as Jesus' opponents helps the T-CR put the disciples between the Pharisees on one side and faithful people such as the Canaanite woman on the other side.

The T-CR has thus been informed of the disciples' limitations and is thereby prepared for the character-shaping incident which follows. The disciples have been presented as witnesses to a variety of different reactions to the positive deeds of Jesus.

Summary

Having reached character-shaping incident five, it is clear that the T-CR has now received a variety of clues important for reaching an understanding of the disciples. The portrayal is becoming more intricate. As the T-CR moves along, the narrative world naturally becomes more expansive and complex. And as the expanded chart for incident five indicates, there are many more responses by the disciples in this central portion of the narrative.

The previous character-shaping incident presented Peter and the disciples through the use of positive and negative responses. After Peter walks on the water, he begins to sink and is called someone with little faith. The incident concludes, however, with the report that the disciples address Jesus as the Son of God, a statement that the T-CR recognizes as consistent with the way Jesus has been portrayed.

The T-CR has, by this point, received assorted information about the disciples and can anticipate more explicit information. It is clear that the disciples rank far above the Pharisees and Sadducees, who continue to be presented negatively — unlike the positive statements allowed in the portrayal of the disciples. The disciples have also been modestly contrasted with the Canaanite woman. But it is clear that she understands the metaphorical language of Jesus' teaching with more perception than the disciples. Metaphorical language has been presented many times to the T-CR as important for the disciples: they were called fishers of people, they are to comprehend the parables, etc.

It is also clear that certain terms and words are being given to the T-CR with more detail. Contrasting the disciples as those of "little faith" with individuals who have "faith" gives the T-CR information with which to comprehend the word "faith." The emphasis in the word is on whether someone can perceive or understand that Jesus can act on behalf of his Father. The few people reported to have "faith" were portrayed as open to the influence of the Father. For the disciples to become "fishers of people," the T-CR requires not only that they follow the Father's son but that they remain open to the implications that may result. Thus the T-CR is receiving more and more of the specifics of the world of this narrative which portray the disciples in a more conglomerate way.

Incident five presents the disciples as having both positive and negative characteristics. The T-CR learns the following about the disciples in the material prior to the incident: (1) that the disciples witness Jesus healing people who recognize him (14:35–36); (2) that they witness Jesus criticizing the Pharisees but are themselves criticized for not understanding his parable about the heart (15:16–20); (3) that they witness another example of an individual with faith whom they did not understand (15:21–28); (4) that they witness Jesus' compassion for the hunger of the large crowd (15:35–38); (5) that they witness more criticism of the Pharisees for their lack of understanding of Jesus (16:1–4).

Within the incident itself, the T-CR is informed in detail that the disciples fail to comprehend Jesus, that they are men of "little faith," but that they did understand Jesus' teaching when he gave them the clue. The *positive* portrayal is clear when Peter repeats what had been stated earlier, that Jesus is the Son of God. Jesus acknowledges Peter's accuracy with the blessing and the more metaphorical imagery of Peter as the rock. However, after adding detail about his (Jesus') status as the son of the Father, Jesus places Peter's rebuke on the side of Satan, opposed to the Father. Peter was open to God's message but within a few moments speaks on behalf of Satan.

Thus the T-CR receives the kind of variation in portrayal that had been presented earlier and that is now contained within one incident. The disciples initially had been portrayed as potentially sensible, dedicated followers who listened to Jesus, but after being taught about what Jesus expected, they are called men of "little faith." After hearing the parables, including some directed at them, the disciples claimed to be capable of understanding Jesus' words, and Jesus seemed to accept their claim. Nevertheless, Jesus described Peter as one of "little faith" when he could not continue to walk on the water. The disciples are reported to have learned from this experience the reality of Jesus' status as son of the Father.

The information conveyed to the T-CR is that Peter and the disciples cannot, no matter how hard they work, arrive at the goal without the assistance of the Father. As Jesus is portrayed as the obedient son, the disciples are portrayed as having reached a significant height, not through their own insight or strength, but through openness to the influence of the Father. Although often portrayed as unable to fulfill Jesus' expectations, the disciples, helped by some positive responses, continue as followers of Jesus.

Character-Shaping Incident Six:

THE DISCIPLES' EXPERIENCE OF THE TRANSFIGURATION OF JESUS
Matt. 17:1–13

INCIDENT SIX (17:1–13) is separated from incident five (16:5–23), by only one paragraph of five verses (16:24–28). The primary feature in the incident is Jesus' transfiguration. However, the narrator does not report it as a direct activity of Jesus, such as a miracle, a teaching, or a dialogue. Chart 6, therefore, shows this incident as the disciples' response to a depiction of Jesus that does not fall into these three categories. The exact classification of the incident will be discussed in the following section. The chart also shows that much of this portion of Matthew's story involves Jesus in dialogue with the disciples, and that it contains a series of the disciples' responses.

Details of Event

This complex incident closely follows after character-shaping incident five, the previous major response to Jesus' question about his identity. Three disciples, Peter, James, and John, are reported to have an unusual experience on a high mountain and, after Peter speaks, are addressed from "the cloud." The narrator portrays the characters in more detail as they come down from the mountain, while they speak with Jesus.

¹And after six days Jesus took with him Peter and James and John his brother, and led them up a high mountain apart. ²And he was transfigured before them, and his face shone like the sun, and his garments became white as light. ³And behold, there appeared to them Moses and Elijah, talking with him. ⁴And Peter said to Jesus, "Lord, it is well that we are here; if you wish, I will make three booths here, one for you and one for Moses and one for Elijah." ⁵He was still speaking, when lo, a bright cloud overshadowed them, and a voice from the cloud said, "This is my beloved Son,

78

Disciple Character-Shaping Analysis #6: Matthew 17:1–13
Expanded Section: Matthew 16:21–17:23

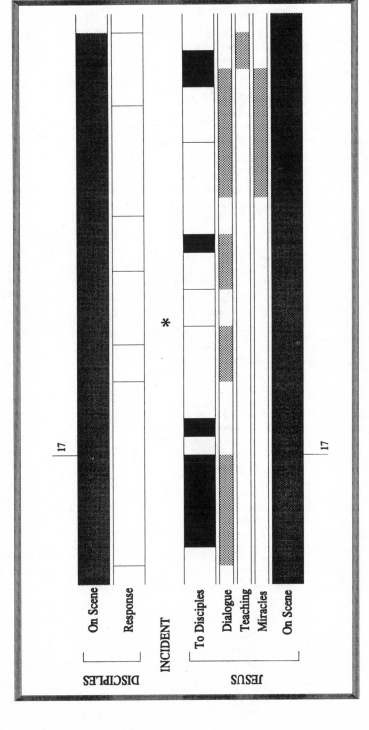

with whom I am well pleased; listen to him." [6]When the disciples heard this, they fell on their faces, and were terribly afraid. [7]But Jesus came and touched them, saying, "Rise, have no fear." [8]And when they lifted up their eyes, they saw no one but Jesus only. [9]And as they were coming down the mountain, Jesus commanded them, "Tell no one the vision, until the Son of Man is raised from the dead." [10]And the disciples asked him, "Then why do the scribes say that first Elijah must come?" [11]He replied, "Elijah does come, and he is to restore all things; [12]but I tell you that Elijah has already come, and they did not know him, but did to him whatever they pleased. So also the Son of Man will suffer at their hands." [13]Then the disciples understood that he was speaking to them of John the Baptist.

This is an unusual incident in this narrative world. It begins with the narrator emphasizing that Jesus, Peter, James, and John are separated from the other disciples and followers. Then he reports what Peter, James, and John witness rather than describing what occurred: "He was transfigured before them...[and] there appeared to them Moses and Elijah..." (17:2–3). The narrator reports the experience of three disciples rather than Jesus' action; he later quotes Jesus referring to this experience as a "vision" (17:19). The narrator acts in the omniscient mode, reporting what occurs in the minds of characters, which is seldom done in this narrative world.

The order of events is important in understanding the way this incident is presented to the T-CR. Peter's response to the experience, as a spokesperson for the three disciples, comes after the narrator's description of the transfiguration. Peter's statement thereby provides the information for the T-CR's understanding of the disciples.

Since the word "transfigure" has not been used before in Matthew's narrative world, the narrator defines the word by using metaphorical language ("his face shone like the sun") and by adding that Jesus was transfigured "before them," to emphasize that the event is primarily the disciples' experience. In addition, it is important for the T-CR when the narrator states that the disciples "see" two individuals, Moses and Elijah, talking to Jesus. Therefore, the narrator does not present the event as an action that he has witnessed, and that he now describes to the narratee, but as an experience in the minds of the three disciples. The narrator reports what the disciples see; the transfiguration is not presented as a specific, definite event.

The T-CR then receives more specific information about what is happening in the minds of the disciples with the report of Peter's response and its interruption. Given the narrator's emphasis on the experience of the disciples, Peter, James, and John are said to see Jesus' face and garments shining brilliantly, and to see that he is also speaking to Moses and Elijah.

With the narrative world, Moses is mentioned in 8:4 as one who commands how people respond to God's actions. Elijah is equated with John the Baptist in chapter 11; also, the disciples report that others believe that Jesus is Elijah (16:14). Thus, both Moses and Elijah are presented as individuals important to the Father. They thereby help the T-CR comprehend the importance of the disciples' experience of the transfiguration of the Son of God.

Peter's statement shows that he recognizes the significance of what he has experienced: "Lord, it is well that we are here; if you wish, I will make three booths here, one for you and one for Moses and one for Elijah" (17:4). The narrator reports Peter's gratitude for being one of the three chosen to see this transfigured image; therefore, Peter seeks to indicate the event's importance — by making booths, that is, places of remembrance — if Jesus wishes. At this point, Peter is portrayed for the T-CR as one who realizes the importance of his experience and who wishes to express his appreciation.

Despite this fact, the weightlessness of Peter's comment becomes clear when the narrator informs the T-CR that, while Peter is speaking, a bright cloud "overshadowed them" and that a voice interrupts Peter: "He was still speaking, when..." (17:5). Thus, although Peter may have intended to say more, he is silenced. The three disciples appear to recognize the implications of the authority revealed in the word from heaven when the narrator reports that they fall on their faces and are greatly afraid.

For the T-CR the most noteworthy feature is that Peter is interrupted by a voice from the cloud ("This is my beloved son, with whom I am well pleased; listen to him," 17:5). The situation brings to the foreground Jesus' baptism, reported in the story's framework. At the baptism, Jesus' Father affirms the data previously presented about Jesus as the Son of God. At the transfiguration, the importance of the disciples' experience is not only in recognizing Jesus' status as the Son of God but, having followed him and heard his teaching, in being commanded to listen to him. Jesus' teaching has been presented to the T-CR as important, but the disciples have not always been able to comprehend — especially his statement about suffering, dying, and rising.

Just as Peter spoke on behalf of the disciples in incident five, he is again the spokesperson for these three disciples. After being portrayed both positively and negatively in incident five, a similar doubleness appears here. That he acknowledges the importance of the incident for all three followers is of minor significance for the T-CR. It is the focus on Peter that seems especially important — once again he is a double-level individual. Thus God's message to the disciples expands: not only is Jesus identified as his son, he is the one whose teaching is of primary importance; his teaching is consistent with the Father's will.

The incident continues when Jesus responds by touching the disciples and addressing them, saying, "Rise, have no fear" (17:7). Again, fear appears as a negative trait of the disciples. The T-CR has seen the word "fear" used in a variety of ways, but when used in reference to the disciples, it is negative. Jesus has told them they are not to fear (10:26, 28; 10:31; 14:27), and fear was identified as the source of Peter's trouble when he sank into the sea (14:30).

After Jesus speaks to the three disciples, the narrator reports what the disciples *now* see: no one but Jesus. Since the narrator does not report the transfiguration as an event but as the disciples' experience, it is their limited perception that records the shining of Jesus' face, the brightness of his garments, and the appearance of Moses and Elijah. Peter's words to Jesus indicate that he recognizes the three figures and that he understands his experience as significant — enough to build three tents or booths for Jesus, Moses, and Elijah.

Therefore in this incident the T-CR first sees Peter as one who reacts too quickly and then whose response is apparently out of place or irrelevant. But the precise limitation of Peter's statement is not clarified within the text. The T-CR is left with another complex portrait of Peter which is both positive and negative.

The conclusion of the incident takes place on the way back from the high mountain, as the group returns to the other disciples. Jesus commands that Peter, James, and John tell no one about the "vision" (17:9) until the Son of Man is raised from the dead, a direct reference to Jesus' statement in the previous incident (16:21). The word "vision" is another new word for the T-CR and reinforces the way the disciples' experience is reported — it was their "seeing" that is being portrayed, their experience. But now the effect of the experience upon the three disciples is to ask Jesus a question: "Then why do the scribes say that first Elijah must come?" Their question makes it clear that they are concerned about the order of events, that is, that they are concerned about the meaning of Jesus' use of the word "until." Since Jesus responds immediately, on the assumption that their question is sensible, the T-CR gets the impression that these three disciples have, in raising the question, understood the basic issue. Jesus answers by making a further point about the order of events. The sequence — Elijah does come → Elijah has already come → therefore the Son of Man will suffer — reaffirms the implication that the incident deals with the timing of events.

This incident concludes with the narrator reporting how the disciples understood the *implication* of Jesus' statement: that Jesus was speaking about John the Baptist. The connection between Elijah and John the Baptist had been stated previously when Jesus explained the importance of John the Baptist: "He is Elijah who is to come" (11:14). However, the disciples had not been "on scene" when that statement was made. But although John the Baptist has been killed by Herod (14:1–12), the T-CR was informed in 16:14 that some understood Jesus to be John the Baptist. The narrator, therefore, informs the T-CR of the comprehension and high status of these three disciples.

Thus, in this event, a subgroup of the disciples is portrayed as making progress in comprehending Jesus' message and situation. Although Peter is interrupted by the Father, represented by the cloud and the voice from heaven, by the end of the incident it is clear these three disciples have profited from their experience. Since the message from the cloud begins with the same statement spoken at Jesus' baptism, it is clear that the early chapters of the narrative—the framework—have helped the T-CR understand who is speaking. The added command, "Listen to him," emphasizes the importance of Jesus' words and makes the question of the disciples a sensible, productive reply. The result for the T-CR is a positive view of these three disciples, provided they continue to listen to Jesus.

Immediate Context

Because there is only one paragraph between incidents five and six, the context for this incident is the immediate context. In character-shaping incident five (16:5–23), after Jesus' praise and criticism of Peter — the person influenced by both God and Satan and who was described at the conclusion as a representative of Satan rather than God — the narrator reports that Jesus teaches his disciples (16:24–28). Jesus begins with a conditional clause ("If any man would come after me...," 16:24), which indicates that the teaching relates directly to the previous event, because it continues to focus on Jesus' comprehension of his future. Therefore, Jesus is expressing his expectations about followers and directs the teaching to the disciples.

The speech is simply organized. It consists of a thesis followed by three reasons/illustrations, which help explain the speech's rationale, and a conclusion which informs the T-CR of its intent. It begins with a conditional clause ("If any man would come after me") and the implications ("let him deny himself and take up his cross and follow me," 16:24). This definition is followed by three "for" (*gar*) clauses verifying the truth and reliability of the thesis. The speech concludes with a statement of the implication of these teachings: "Truly I say to you, there are some standing here who will not taste death before they see the Son of Man coming in his kingdom" (16:28). The statement aims to influence the listeners (disciples) and to state the effect such actions would have on their fate.

The initial "thesis" statement says followers must deny themselves, take up their cross, and follow Jesus (16:24). The word "cross" has been used once before (10:38), in the speech focusing on the persecution of the disciples, which was directed to the disciples only. In this statement the actions required of a responsive follower are similar in intent, i.e., they emphasize the positive *action*, not passive reception, of the true follower. Jesus' statement about his suffering, death, and resurrection indicates the danger involved in following him, but since there is little information provided about the incident's meaning, the T-CR is confronted with a gap. But the phrase "follow me" is now gaining a more detailed explanation in the sense that following Jesus may also lead to one's death and renewal.

The first "for" explanation ("For whoever would save his life will lose it, and whoever loses his life for my sake will find it," 16:25) repeats, in different terms, the thesis statement: losing a life will result in finding life. The second explanation ("For what will it profit a man, if he gains the whole world and forfeits his life?" 16:26) uses two rhetorical questions to address the same topic. Saving one's life is the primary goal. The third explanation moves to the future by stating, "For the Son of Man is to come with his angels in the glory of his Father, and then he will repay every man for what he has done" (16:27). The concluding affirmative statement, "Truly I say to you, there are some standing here who will not taste death before they see the Son of Man coming in his kingdom" (17:28), continues to focus on the future and predicts the survival of some "standing here," that is, disciples.

There is no report of the disciples' reaction to Jesus' teaching or of how they comprehend it. All the T-CR receives is the statement at the beginning of incident six, saying that six days later Jesus took Peter, James, and John to the mountain. Despite Jesus' short teaching about the validity of his statement of death and resurrection, the T-CR does not learn how the disciples might have understood it. But when the Father commands them to "listen to him," the T-CR is informed that to be a disciple is to listen and understand both who Jesus is and how his death and resurrection form part of his positive action as the son of the Father.

Summary

The T-CR continues to be informed about the followers initially "called" to become "fishers of people." The T-CR has learned in detail about Jesus' expectations of the disciples. And the disciples have been portrayed as limited individuals who nonetheless seem to move in the right direction. They are men of little faith rather than men of no faith. But when people with faith are portrayed, the limitations of the disciples become obvious.

At this point in the story, having been exposed to more information about Jesus, the T-CR receives clear information about the growing number of Jesus' opponents. As a result, the positive element of the disciples is strengthened.

The proximity of character-shaping incidents five and six emphasizes the complex character of one of the disciples, Peter. He is honored by Jesus in a distinctive way because of his openness to the Father, but the T-CR then witnesses Jesus' equally distinctive rebuke because, when confronted by new information about Jesus as the suffering Son of God, Peter is unable to accept it.

The "transfiguration" provides deeper insight about the experience of three of the disciples and their progress toward becoming proper followers of Jesus. The T-CR has been given more detailed information about the disciples. The recognition, by three disciples, of Jesus as one in verbal contact with two of the Father's important workers, Moses and Elijah, is positive but lessens in importance when Peter is interrupted by the voice from the cloud. It is the Father himself who repeats his statement identifying Jesus as his son and commanding the disciples that, given the experience, their primary responsibility as a follower is to *listen* to Jesus. For the T-CR much of Jesus' earlier teaching was intended for the education of the disciples; now he shifts to present his true identity — as the Son of Man who must suffer, die, and be raised. The "vision" of the transfiguration must not be told to others *until* the Son of Man has risen. The T-CR learns that these three disciples are capable of a clear understanding of Jesus' teaching. In this case, the narrator says, they recognize John the Baptist not only as the one who prepares Jesus' way but as one whose fate bears similarities to Jesus' fate.

The information the T-CR gains about the disciples thus resembles information provided in previous incidents. They are seen as far from ideal followers, but they make progress toward fulfilling Jesus' expectations. Nevertheless, when the three disciples experience Jesus' transfiguration, the T-CR learns that the Father reaffirms Jesus' status as his beloved son and as one whose teaching must also be comprehended by those who follow. For the T-CR at this point in the narrative world, a disciple is an intent follower of Jesus, but one who does not yet fulfill Jesus' expectations. The disciples continue to receive information from the Father but have not acted as expected.

Character-Shaping Incident Seven:

THE DIALOGUE ABOUT RICHES
Matt. 19:23–20:28

INCIDENT SEVEN is much longer than any previous character-shaping incident and therefore gives the T-CR more complex information. As the expanded chart demonstrates, the context of incident seven contains a lengthy section of dialogue from Jesus. Almost all of Jesus' activity is directed to, or in the presence of, the disciples; as a result, there is more material with which to understand the incident's impact on the T-CR. The T-CR continues to be informed in this incident of Jesus' expectations of the disciples and receives more details for comprehending their portrait.

Details of Event

There are two related sections in this character-shaping incident. The first section is a dialogue between Jesus and the disciples about what it means to be saved; it begins with Jesus' statement about the difficulty the rich will encounter entering the kingdom of heaven (19:23–24) and ends with a parable about laborers in a vineyard (20:1–16). Section two, following immediately, begins with Jesus' statement about his purpose in going to Jerusalem (20:17–19), continues with a dialogue with the disciples and one of their relatives (20:20–24), and concludes with Jesus' statement about the significance of the death of the Son of Man (20:25–28).

> ²³And Jesus said to his disciples, "Truly, I say to you, it will be hard for a rich man to enter the kingdom of heaven. ²⁴Again, I tell you, it is easier for a camel to go through the eye of a needle than for a rich man to enter the kingdom of God." ²⁵When the disciples heard this they were greatly astonished, saying, "Who then can be saved?" ²⁶But Jesus looked at them and said to them, "With men this is impossible, but with God all things are possible." ²⁷Then Peter said in reply, "Lo, we have left everything and followed you. What then shall we have?" ²⁸Jesus said to them, "Truly, I say to

86

Disciple Character-Shaping Analysis #7: Matthew 19:23–20:28
Expanded Section: Matthew 17:14–20:28

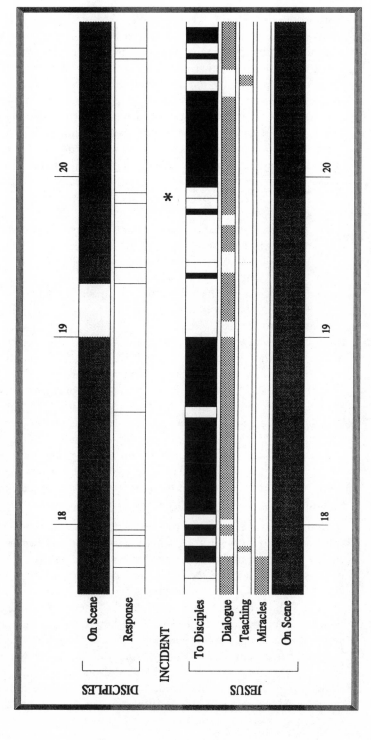

you, in the new world, when the Son of Man shall sit on his glo-
rious throne, you who have followed me will also sit on twelve
thrones, judging the twelve tribes of Israel. [29]And everyone who
has left houses or brothers or sisters or father or mother or children or lands, for my name's sake, will receive a hundred-fold,
and inherit eternal life. [30]But many that are first will be last, and
the last first. [20:1]For the kingdom of heaven is like a householder
who went out early in the morning to hire laborers for his vineyard. [2]After agreeing with the laborers for a denarius a day, he
sent them into his vineyard. [3]And going out about the third hour
he saw others standing idle in the market place; [4]and to them he
said, 'You go into the vineyard too, and whatever is right I will give
you.' So they went. [5]Going out again about the sixth hour and the
ninth hour, he did the same. [6]And about the eleventh hour he went
out and found others standing; and he said to them, 'Why do you
stand here idle all day?' [7]They said to him, 'Because no one has
hired us.' He said to them, 'You go into the vineyard too.' [8]And
when evening came, the owner of the vineyard said to he stew-
ard, 'Call the laborers and pay them their wages, beginning with
the last, up to the first.' [9]And when those hired about the eleventh
hour came, each of them received a denarius. [10]Now when the first
came, they thought they would receive more; but each of them
also received a denarius. [11]And on receiving it they grumbled at
the householder, [12]saying, 'These last worked only one hour, and
you have made them equal to us who have borne the burden of
the day and the scorching heat.' [13]But he replied to one of them,
"Friend, I am doing you no wrong; did you not agree with me for
a denarius? [14]Take what belongs to you, and go; I choose to give to
this last as I give to you. [15]Am I not allowed to do what I choose
with what belongs to me? Or do you begrudge my generosity?'
[16]So the last will be first, and the first last."

[17]And as Jesus was going up to Jerusalem, he took the twelve disciples aside, and on the way he said to them, [18]"Behold, we are going
up to Jerusalem; and the Son of Man will be delivered to the chief
priests and scribes, and they will condemn him to death, [19]and deliver him to the Gentiles to be mocked and scourged and crucified,
and he will be raised on the third day." [20]Then the mother of the
sons of Zebedee came up to him with her sons, and kneeling before him she asked him for something. [21]And he said to her, "What
do you want?" She said to him, "Command that these two sons of
mine may sit, one at your right hand and one at you left, in your
kingdom." [22]But Jesus answered, "You [plural] do not know what
you are asking. Are you able to drink the cup that I am to drink?"

They said to him, "We are able." [23]He said to them, "You will drink my cup, but to sit at my right hand and at my left is not mine to grant, but it is for those for whom it has been prepared by my Father." [24]And when the ten heard it, they were indignant at the two brothers. [25]But Jesus called them to him and said, "You know that the rulers of the Gentiles lord it over them, and their great men exercise authority over them. [26]It shall not be so among you; but whoever would be great among you must be your servant, [27]and whoever would be first among you must be your slave; [28]even as the Son of Man came not to be served but to serve, and to give his life as a ransom for many."

This character-shaping incident begins with Jesus' statement to the disciples (19:23–24) following his conversation with a rich "young man" (19:16–22.) Therefore the T-CR is informed that Jesus is explaining, drawing the implications, and reinforcing the significance of this previous encounter for the edification of the disciples. The introductory term "truly" has been used often by Jesus and helps indicate the importance of the statement which ends with a metaphorical comparison, in involving a camel going through the eye of a needle. The narrator reports the disciples' response to the statement/comparison as "greatly astonished." They say, "Who then can be saved?" (19:25). Thus the T-CR is shown that their response focuses on entering the kingdom rather than the metaphor that Jesus used to state his point. Within the context, the disciples' question is comprehensible, especially since Jesus had phrased his comparison to imply that a rich man, with difficulty, could enter the kingdom. The disciples understood Jesus' metaphor because they asked about "being saved" as another way of speaking about entering the kingdom of God.

The T-CR has of course been informed about the kingdom. The phrase "kingdom of heaven" has been used often prior to this incident: (1) in the framework as the basic topic of John the Baptist and of Jesus (3:2; 4:17); (2) as a primary item in the thesis statement and in other places in Jesus' first teaching (5:3, 10, 19, 20; 6:33; 7:21); (3) and frequently when Jesus speaks to the disciples. The phrase appears in incident three in Jesus' response to the disciples' positive answer about understanding the parables, and also as part of the explanation of the parable, and in incident five in which the keys of the kingdom are promised to Peter. Now here in incident seven the phrase is used three times, and heavily emphasized. Thus the T-CR has been informed of the significance of the kingdom for Jesus and his expectations of the disciples. When the disciples indicate that being saved is a way of talking about entering the kingdom of God, Jesus' response is positive — they have asked a comprehensible question.

The word "save" has also been given meaning for the T-CR. In the framework of the narrative, the angel of the Lord tells Joseph that Mary's child is to be called Jesus "for (*gar*) he will save his people from their sins" (1:21). Thus the T-CR was informed that saving people is an important way to understand Jesus' task. In character-shaping incident two, the disciples ask to be saved from the storm, and they are. Similarly, Peter, in incident four, when he sinks into the sea after walking upon it, is saved. Saving is also connected to Jesus' healing of the woman with a hemorrhage (9:21–22). However, in Jesus' teaching to the disciples about their role as apostles, Jesus' statement ("he who endures to the end will be saved," 10:22) adds a wider meaning to the word "saved." But, when Jesus speaks about his death and resurrection, he tells the disciples that one cannot save himself unless he loses his life "for my sake" (16:25). Thus, "save" has been used to speak of a time beyond the present life, after one's death. Therefore the T-CR has been informed of many meanings for the word "save." It is clear that the disciples comprehend the meaning of entering the kingdom of heaven. But they have not comprehended Jesus' new message, which began in chapter 16, about the significance of his death, and of following him as a way of being saved.

Jesus' response ("With men this is impossible, but with God all things are possible," 19:26), therefore, is consistent with his earlier statements. The narrator makes explicit that he directs his response to the disciples. The statement itself confirms the implication in the change of the voice of the verb. God is the one who saves; people do not *save themselves*. Since the T-CR consistently sees the impact of the Father's action upon everyone in the story, the statement brings to the foreground the earlier emphasis of the Father's role.

Peter then continues the conversation (19:27). His statement about the disciples' actions ("leaving everything and following Jesus") is consistent with the details of the story presented to the T-CR to this point. Peter's statement reveals that, for him, "following" means a thorough modification of one's way of life. Thus his question, "What then shall we have?" (19:27), indicates concern about his fate. Peter, however, seems to interpret "following" with more flexibility than the expectations Jesus had already revealed. Peter's initial statement shows the T-CR that he may agree with Jesus' expectations. But his question, "What then shall we have?" shows he does not understand the implications of Jesus' recent emphasis on death as a possible result of following the Son of Man.

That Jesus continues the conversation shows that he recognizes the significance of the question. The first part of his response (19:28–30) focuses on the point of Peter's question: "What then shall we have?" Jesus begins by describing the situation in the "new world" and acknowledging that the followers will have a special responsibility to judge the twelve tribes of Israel. This is a task they had not been informed about previously. For the T-CR Jesus' statement means that they will have high responsibility; it seems to be a positive response. But Jesus continues by indicating that "following," which Peter emphasized, has positive results for others, not just the disciples. For anyone who acts in a similar way, by leaving family or land, following can lead to eternal life if it is "for my name's sake." Thus the T-CR is informed of some more specifics of Jesus' expectation of the disciples. Jesus agrees with Peter that leaving everything is indeed an important part of following, but the major point is the *reason* that one leaves everything: "for my name's sake" (19:29).

The T-CR also receives significant information about the word "name." Although the word was used initially to refer to what Jesus is to be called, Jesus is also said to be equated with the name Emmanuel (1:23). A "name" thus appears to be more than a label; it also indicates a person's reality or the source of his life. Jesus later used the word "name" to refer to the Father, a way of acknowledging who God is (6:9). Also in the second major teaching of the disciples, chapter 10, he tells them, "You will be hated for my name's sake" (10:22), and that some individuals will be received based on who they really are (10:41–42). In addition, in a quote from Isaiah, God is referred to with the word "name": "And in his name will the Gentiles hope" (12:21). In the teaching of the disciples in chapter 18, Jesus describes certain actions positively, such as receiving children or gathering together, *if* the action is done "in my name" (18:5, 20). When used here in incident seven, "in my name" continues to focus on the phrase's common use in this narrative world — which means "based on who he really is." Jesus has been emphasizing the significance of his fate — death and resurrection — and used the title "Son of Man" in conjunction with it. So, for the T-CR, the use of the word "name" in incident seven has been consistent. To follow Jesus is to know his name, who he really is: the Son of God and the Son of Man who will die and rise.

Therefore, Jesus' point, in response to Peter's question, is that leaving everything is indeed important, but more important is the reason for the action. If one leaves because of who Jesus is, then the implication is that some who "follow" Jesus may not be prepared to stay with him to his death and resurrection. Those who seem to be his followers now might not continue to follow. God's decision about who will be saved is not based on what appears to Peter as the primary determinant — leaving everything and following — but on such action performed *because of who he is,* the son who is to die and rise.

When Jesus concludes this part of his response with a comparative affirmation, "but many that are first will be last, and the last first" (19:30), its meaning in this incident is clear for the T-CR. Since the discussion has centered on those who have riches in contrast to those who have left everything, those who "are first" refers to those who have high status in the world now, and therefore may indeed be last in the future.

Having made this comparative statement, Jesus continues his response to Peter's question about what the disciples shall have with a parable, another metaphoric comparison (20:1–16). The parable begins with "for" (*gar*) and thus functions as an explanation of the previous statement ("But many that are first will be last, and the last first," 19:30) and its relation to the earlier reference to the kingdom of God. The parable focuses on the complaint of the twelve-hour workers about being paid at a rate far below those who worked less than twelve hours; they claim to have earned more because they have "borne the burden of the day and the scorching heat" (20:12). The parable ends with a response by the householder. After addressing the situation directly he concludes by asking, "Do you begrudge my generosity? [Literally: Is your eye evil because I am good (generous)?] So the last will be first, and the first last" (20:15–16). This parable says the problem does not involve the distribution of money or riches but God's graciousness. Certain human business principles of control and justice should not be applied to issues concerning the kingdom of heaven. Thus there is a continuing depredation of the disciples. It is not based on what they do but whether they do so because of who he is, because of his "name."

Since the disciples are not reported to respond, the T-CR has no indication that they understand the parable, although they had been presented earlier as capable, in a limited way, of understanding such teaching. But the narrator continues (20:17) by reporting that Jesus speaks to them again later. He repeats the prediction of his fate in Jerusalem, and thus the importance of this new teaching for the disciples is underlined for the T-CR. Then the narrator reports that the mother of James and John requests that her sons receive places of authority "in your kingdom." Since Jesus' statement was directed to "the twelve disciples" (20:17) it is not reported to the T-CR why she asks her question. However, with her reference to the kingdom, the T-CR sees her emphasis on the use of the power of the kingdom by her sons and not the significance of Jesus' "name" or fate. She is acting similar to a "rich" person, one of the first who will be last. She wants verification of the earlier proclamation that the disciples "who follow" will sit on the throne. Thus the T-CR gets a slightly negative view of the mother.

Rather than speaking directly to this woman, Jesus asks her sons if they are able to drink the cup that "I am to drink" (20:22), a metaphor which emphasizes the importance of Jesus' just-stated fate, his prediction of his death and resurrection. The response of James and John is direct: "We are able" (20:22). Jesus' reply to their quick acceptance of responsibility tells them they will indeed drink his cup, and yet it is the Father, not Jesus, who grants places of authority "for those for whom it has been prepared by my Father" (20:23). Thus Jesus emphasizes, again, that he recognizes the authority of his Father; the Father is the source of salvation. The disciples' fate is determined by God, despite their actions. For the T-CR Jesus' statement refers to the generosity of the householder in the parable. Again, there is no reported response from James and John, and therefore the T-CR is not informed if they understand or accept their possible persecution and death.

The narrator reports that the other ten disciples are indignant toward the two brothers (20:24). Since the narrator does not state the cause of their indignation, the T-CR encounters another gap in understanding their thoughts. But Jesus continues to emphasize the primary message — the reversal of usual positions — by drawing a comparison to a social situation: be a servant to be great, be a slave to be first (20:25–28). The concluding statement concerns his own fate. The Son of Man came to serve and give his life as a ransom for many (20:28).

The repeated emphasis on Jesus' fate and its significance reemphasizes for the T-CR the limited portrayal of the disciples presented in this incident. Jesus appears as a teacher whose words are taken seriously, and whose implications are considered carefully by the disciples. Jesus is not portrayed as responding sarcastically or negatively; he recognizes the validity of the disciples' comments and attempts to answer them forthrightly. The disciples' interest in their own position is not based on unrealistic expectations but on a legitimate concern for the impact of their self-sacrifice as followers. They are depicted as closer to the rich man and others who use social status and achievements as an indication of their worth. But according to Jesus, if the disciples wish to enter the kingdom they must be ready for experiences that appear drastic, but which could lead to the positive end of salvation. To follow Jesus as the Son of Man requires that one recognize who he really is and realize that life may end in a troubling way. One must follow him because of his "name."

Context

The narrative between character-shaping incident six (17:1–13) and seven (19:23–20:28) continues to focus on the disciples and consists primarily of sayings of Jesus.

There are seven sections (A through F, and the immediate context) in this narrative interval. The disciples are present in almost every incident, sometimes asking questions, sometimes directly addressed. Thus there is more information for the T-CR about Jesus' expectations and about his emphasis on the disciples' limits.

A. Based on the narrator's emphasis at the conclusion of incident six, that the disciples understood Jesus' implications about John the Baptist as Elijah (17:13), the T-CR has received a positive impression about the disciples' progress toward fulfilling the expectations of Jesus. Section A (17:14–20), however, now raises questions about their ability to accomplish what Jesus has requested. An unnamed man appeals to Jesus to heal his epileptic son and reports that the disciples could not heal him. Jesus responds by addressing the "faithless and perverse generation," which must be the nine disciples, with a rhetorical question about the frustration this faithless and perverse generation causes. This specific phrase had not been used before. The word "generation" has been used a number of times in a general way; the word "perverse" has not been used before; "faithless" was used once by Jesus to describe the people of his own country (13:58). However, the words "faith" and "little faith" have been supplied more specific content. The disciples have been called people of "little faith" five times. Thus the T-CR is informed of Jesus' critical response. The question, "How long am I to be with you?" (17:17) also gives the T-CR information about Jesus' criticism. Then the narrator reports that Jesus immediately rebukes the demon.

Having been heavily criticized by Jesus, the disciples ask a question which demonstrates their concern: "Why could we not cast it out?" (17:19). The T-CR is thereby informed that the nine disciples had attempted to heal, as Jesus had recommended. Jesus' answer continues the previous criticisms: "Because of your little faith" (17:20). He concludes with a metaphor about how faith could move a mountain; with faith, nothing would be impossible. Therefore, the T-CR is clearly informed of the weight of Jesus' criticism of the disciples, even though the narrator has reported their increasing ability to understand some of the images and implications of Jesus' message. Their problem is their faith, not their comprehension; they may understand what is required but cannot, as yet, act in a way that meets Jesus' expectation.

The T-CR has been informed of "faith" often, and therefore use of the word is important in comprehending the disciples. "Faith" has appeared 12 times previously, and in all but two instances was spoken by Jesus. When the narrator used the word, he reported that Jesus "saw" the faith of people who sought his help for a sick person (9:2) and that Jesus did not do many mighty works because of the unbelief of the people in his "own country" (13:58). In every instance that "faith" appeared in this narrative world, it was addressed either to the disciples or spoken in their presence. Therefore the T-CR knows its importance in understanding the disciples.

The first use of "faith" occurred in Jesus' initial teaching of the disciples (6:30), in which he warns the disciples not to be anxious, "O men of little faith." The opposite of anxiousness requires one to "seek first his kingdom and his righteousness" (6:33). Thus Jesus anticipates the disciples' limitations. In contrast, Jesus twice declares the faith of the centurion who asks for Jesus' aid and recognizes his authority (8:10, 13). Shortly thereafter, in 8:26, Jesus again describes the disciples as those with "little faith" in character-shaping incident two. In three different incidents in chapter 9, a group of people, the woman with a hemorrhage, and the two blind men are identified as having faith — all because they act in a way that shows they recognize the authority or power that Jesus possesses. Peter is addressed as having "little faith" in incident four when he is afraid. The Canaanite woman is said to have faith because she recognizes Jesus' authority and comprehends his metaphorical response (15:28). In 16:8 the disciples again are addressed as having "little faith" because they do not understand Jesus' metaphorical teaching about the leaven of the Pharisees.

Therefore, having previously demonstrated to the T-CR the "little faith" of the disciples, Jesus calls the nine "faithless and perverse" when they are unable to cure the man's son. This is the only time the word "perverse' appears in this story. Thus it does not help the T-CR gain insight into Jesus' description of the disciples.

The result for the T-CR, therefore, is criticism of the disciples. After a relatively positive portrayal of the three, Peter, James, and John, in character-shaping incident six at the transfiguration, the nine are heavily denounced as having no faith. The T-CR thus receives further information to back up the previous criticism of Jesus. But Jesus has not given up on the disciples, and his final statement ("For truly I say to you, if you have faith as a grain of mustard seed, you will say to this mountain, 'Move from here to there,' and it will move; and nothing will be impossible to you," 17:20) implies that they might be able to improve. Thus, although Jesus' criticism and the disciples' limitations are clear, Jesus' hope continues — the fulfillment of his expectations is still possible.

B. The narrator then reports that Jesus tells the disciples about his fate (17:22–23). The first mention of his death and resurrection, in 16:21, was the narrator's summary of Jesus' words; the second prediction consists of a quote from Jesus himself. The T-CR again receives a positive impression of the disciples when the narrator reports that "they were greatly distressed" (17:23) upon hearing Jesus' statement. Thus the movement from positive to negative to positive within a short portion of the narrative helps raise the suspicion and expectation of the T-CR. The disciples are portrayed in both positive and negative ways; they are followers who have not yet achieved the status that Jesus requires. At the same time, the T-CR is given added information about the importance of Jesus' future. The T-CR must anticipate Jesus' future and wonder what impact it will have on the followers.

C. The disciples remain in the foreground in the next section (17:24–27) when Peter answers "yes" to the tax collectors' inquiry about whether Jesus pays the temple tax. When Peter returns home, the narrator reports that Jesus spoke to him "first," with knowledge of what Peter has just said; the account shows that Jesus knew about the inquiry just reported even though he was not present when Peter was questioned. Jesus' response, about how Peter understands kings and their sons, implies that Jesus knows he will be requested to pay the tax. Although Peter is directly involved in this incident, little information is given to the T-CR about Peter himself. After Peter answers that the kings expect tribute "from others" rather than from sons, as one would anticipate, Jesus says, "Then the sons are free" (17:26). To clarify the implications of this conclusion, Jesus instructs Peter to take the shekel from a fish he will catch and to use it to pay the tax for Jesus and himself. The narrator does not report whether Peter obeys; the T-CR knows only the request of Jesus. Thus the incident functions as a parable and does not add significant information to the portrait of Peter. Its purpose is to state the principles that Jesus uses in relation with the authorities and which he expects the disciples to follow: do not offend the temple tax collectors.

D. In the fourth section (18:1–35), the narrator begins by stating that the disciples ask a question "at that time," and the T-CR is thereby informed that there is a direct connection between incidents C and D. The question, "Who is the greatest in the kingdom of heaven?" (18:1), indicates a primary concern among the disciples and their interest in the community of followers. Jesus' response begins with interesting imagery. The disciples ask about greatness and, in explanation, he emphasizes the humility of a child. The following speech further indicates Jesus' expectation for any followers. Now that a new factor about Jesus' fate has received emphasis, the T-CR is informed in more detail about the "little faith" of the disciples which Jesus has expressed repeatedly. By using a child as an example, he indicates the emphasis of the speech that follows and, of course, sets the tone for this (seven) character-shaping incident.

It is important for the T-CR that the humility of the child is stated. Jesus had used this word once before, at the conclusion of chapter 11, when he thanked the Father and stated his understanding of his role as the son: "I am gentle and humble of heart" (11:29). Now the word gains more meaning for the T-CR in application to the child. Greatness in the kingdom is not based on achievement. Status in the kingdom, the point of the question from the disciples, depends on humility.

The remainder of this portion of the speech (18:5–20) elaborates upon the "thesis" statement about humility. Since this portion is addressed directly to the disciples, it expands for the T-CR the details of Jesus' expectations of them. How does one express or demonstrate the required humility? First, Jesus emphasizes reception of "one such child in my name" (18:5) as opposed to causing him to sin. The point becomes clearer in the next clause (18:6) when the child is presented as an image of one who has faith "in me." Again, faith is emphasized. The T-CR is informed to equate "faith" with whoever humbles himself like this child. Causing one to sin is further explained with the example of removing one's hand or foot or eye if those parts of the body cause sin. (18:7–9) The implication is, of course, that the person or disciple who causes someone else to sin will be removed.

The emphasis on the disciples continues with the reference to "little ones," a phrase previously used to describe the disciples or followers. Little ones should not be "despised" (18:10). In addition, Jesus explains the parable of the lost sheep (18:12–13) by stressing that the Father does not want any of these little ones to perish.

The final statements in this first portion of the teaching (18:15–20) elaborate upon the word "perish." Jesus begins with, "If your brother sins . . . ," and continues to explain the process for bringing the person back into the community. In conclusion, the disciples are told that they have the authority to bind and loose, along with the Father. But it is the importance of Jesus as the intermediary that is stressed at the conclusion: "Again I say to you, if two of you agree on earth about anything you ask, it will be done for you by my Father in heaven. For where two or three are gathered in my name, there am I in the midst of them" (18:19–20). In effect, Jesus tells the disciples that they are following him as the representative of the Father. Therefore the T-CR can view the disciples as people with special privileges and responsibilities.

Up to this point, Jesus has explained the disciples' relation to the Father through the Son. Although they will have authoritative positions, the disciples are expected to be humble and open to forgiveness, just as Jesus has demonstrated in his attitude to them, which reflects the Father's attitude. The reference to the assembly (*ekklesia*) of the people repeats the term used from 16:18, where Jesus states he will build his assembly. Establishment of the assembly in 16:18 depends in part upon the disciples' authority.

Jesus' teaching is interrupted by another question from Peter, in response to the previous material: "How often should I forgive?" (18:21). This question indicates to the T-CR that Peter has grasped the implications of Jesus' statement and is moving on to practical problems. Jesus' response, "Forgive not seven but seventy times seven" (18:22), reinforces his expectation of mercy from the disciples. Jesus continues this focus on forgiveness with the parable of a householder who forgives one of his servants an immense debt; the servant, however, does not forgive a small debt from a fellow servant. The parable ends with the conclusion that the Father will punish a follower who does not reflect the humility and forgiveness that must accompany the authority and greatness he has in the kingdom (18:35).

E. A break in time occurs (19:1) with the report that Jesus, after teaching the disciples, leaves Galilee and enters Judea beyond the Jordan where he continues his healing among the crowds. Apparently as a result of this healing activity, the Pharisees test him with a question about divorce (19:3). Jesus answers with a question which uses the same phrase he used earlier when the Pharisees attacked the activities of the disciples: "Have you not read that…" (19:4). He shows them that he draws his conclusion from scripture, not from his own judgment. The Pharisees, therefore, respond with another question which indicates that they can refer to similar material and come to a different conclusion; there is apparently conflict within the source that Jesus uses for his response. Thus the Pharisees are portrayed as determined and clever. Jesus' second reply acknowledges that the principle of unchastity allows divorce, but says Moses granted the exception because of "your hardness of heart" (19:8). Since the narrator does not report a response from the Pharisees, the T-CR is left with another gap. Although it is clear that Jesus does not accept the Pharisees' beliefs about divorce, Jesus also indicates his compliance with the Father, the source of the law, and acknowledges that Moses was dealing with a specific situation (19:8–9). For the T-CR, this situation resembles Jesus' understanding of the law when he taught the disciples in his first educational speech (5:22–48).

This dialogue, then, sets the context for the disciples' next comment: "If such is the case of a man with his wife it is not expedient to marry" (19:10). Since the narrator does not indicate how the Pharisees responded to Jesus' statement, when the disciples are reported to respond the focus has returned to them. The comment indicates that they have understood Jesus' reply but find it hard to apply to their world. In effect, they are asking Jesus to continue the analysis of divorce. His reply indicates, again, his expectations for the disciples: "He who is able to receive (comprehend, grasp) this, let him receive it" (19:12).

F. After this instruction about the impact the Father can have on individuals, the narrator reports that children were brought to Jesus so he could lay his hands on them and pray (19:13). This statement brings to the foreground for the T-CR the thesis of the previous section: the humility of children as a positive characteristic of members of the kingdom. In addition, the narrator emphasizes (19:14) how children are received and how the disciples rebuke the people who brought them (19:13). Jesus' reply is both (1) a rebuke of the disciples for their interference and insensitivity, and (2) a reaffirmation of children as a symbol for members of the kingdom. Thus this portion of the story stresses additional requirements for those who are part of the kingdom. The narrator concludes simply that Jesus laid his hands upon the children and departed. The disciples are thereby portrayed to the T-CR as followers who still have not been able to comprehend all the details about their status and the qualities expected of true followers of Jesus.

Immediate Context

The incident immediately preceding character-shaping incident seven begins with an indefinite identification of "one" who asks: "Teacher, what good deed must I do to have eternal life?" (19:16). Because the questioner is not identified, the emphasis falls on the question and not the questioner. Nevertheless, Jesus' response is concise: he questions the person's intent in using the word "good" by stating, "One there is who is good" (19:17). Jesus gives advice similar to his initial teaching (5:17–20): "Keep the commandments" (19:17). When asked to list the commands he has in mind, Jesus lists six. The narrator then gives the T-CR more information about the questioner. The "young man" replies that he has observed all six commandments but asks what he lacks. Thus the questioner appears confident about his ability to observe some of the Father's major requirements, but at the same time recognizes his inability to carry out all the requirements; he is aware of his limitations but does not understand the "good deed" that he thinks is necessary. In this sense, he is portrayed like the disciples in that he recognizes his limitations but does not know about or comprehend Jesus' expectations.

Jesus' reply is pointed. If you seek perfection, give all your possessions to the poor and follow me (19:21). These requirements were stated earlier in the second major teaching (10:5–42) as necessary for a true disciple. Peter and the followers have given up their jobs to follow Jesus. Within this story, the young man is invited to become one of the followers. The incident ends, however, with the narrator reporting that he went away sorrowfully, because he had great possessions. Thus it is only at the end of the incident that the T-CR is informed by the narrator about the identity of the questioner as a rich young man. The T-CR is told directly that his possessions caused him to turn away and not accept Jesus' demand. Perfection is possible, it seems, for those who give up their wealth and follow Jesus. However, as the T-CR has seen, the disciples, though they apparently have given up their possessions, still have not been able to reach the level of comprehension and faith that Jesus requires. Accompanying Jesus is not the disciples' problem; meeting his expectations as followers has been their difficulty.

Summary

The contextual material between character-shaping incidents six and seven is important. After the transfiguration of incident six, which presents the three disciples somewhat positively and emphasizes the importance of Jesus' teaching, the T-CR is clearly informed of Jesus' criticism of the other nine disciples for not being able to heal the epileptic child (17:17). Their faith is still "little." The focus for the T-CR remains on the disciples as they are informed once again of Jesus' coming death and resurrection, and of his willingness to pay temple taxes. Following the emphasis on listening to his teaching, the narrator provides a longer teaching response by Jesus (18:1–35) in which the disciples ask about greatness in the kingdom of heaven. Jesus emphasizes the importance of humility with examples of other appropriate actions, including receiving others, causing no temptations, caring for people in need, and forgiving.

The T-CR also learns more about Jesus' opponents from the Pharisees' question about divorce and about his continuing emphasis on receiving people, especially children (19:1–15).

Finally, just before this character-shaping incident, the rich man claims to have obeyed the commandments but is not willing to be "perfect," i.e., to sell his possessions and give to the poor (19:16–22).

After this context, Jesus, the son of the Father, turns again to the disciples to stress the heavy requirements of being a follower. Given their limited reaction, the portrait the T-CR receives of the disciples continues to become more complex. The disciples have been taught in many different ways. They have been informed of Jesus' expectations and now receive more information about his fate and the potential results of following a persecuted leader. They are portrayed more positively than opponents, but continue to be shown as followers with little faith. A disciple listens but does not always comprehend. They are moving in a positive direction but not making much progress.

In this incident, then, in which the disciples are specifically portrayed, they raise a significant question ("Who then can be saved?" 19:25) in response to Jesus' statement ("It will be hard for a rich man to enter the kingdom of heaven," 19:23) with its metaphor of a camel going through the eye of a needle. During the conversation, the T-CR is informed of a specific, positive self-evaluation from Peter about the disciples having left everything in order to follow Jesus. In response, Jesus emphasizes not the action itself but the reason for such action: "for my name's sake." His name expresses his reality; the emphasis falls on his fate, in the future, and not on his teaching or actions in the past.

After using another metaphor to educate the disciples, Jesus repeats the passion prediction and emphasizes both the importance of humility and the significance of understanding his "name." His expectations are elaborated. Although the disciples are rebuked for their attitude toward the children, characterized as humble, they are contrasted positively with the Pharisees.

For the T-CR, the narrative stresses that perfection equals giving up wealth, as the disciples did, and emphasizes the limited capability of the disciples. The result for the T-CR is positive, in a limited way. The disciples are followers of Jesus but, although they have improved their comprehension of Jesus, they have not yet reached his expectations.

Character-Shaping Incident Eight:

JUDAS ISCARIOT BECOMES
THE BETRAYER
Matt. 26:14–25

INCIDENT EIGHT has the longest context among the eleven, that is, the longest narrative segment between incidents. As the expanded chart shows, Jesus' activity primarily involves teaching and dialogue; the character-shaping incident consists of the disciples' response to the dialogue. This section also contains the largest portion of the story in which the disciples are not "on scene."

Details of Event

Judas, one of the chosen twelve, identified by the narrator as a betrayer (10:4), agrees to "deliver" Jesus to the chief priests and later is confronted by Jesus at the Last Supper.

[14]Then one of the twelve, who was called Judas Iscariot, went to the chief priests [15]and said, "What will you give me if I deliver him to you?" And they paid him thirty pieces of silver. [16]And from that moment he sought an opportunity to betray him. [17]Now on the first day of Unleavened Bread the disciples came to Jesus, saying, "Where will you have us prepare for you to eat the Passover?" [18]He said, "Go into the city to a certain one, and say to him, 'The Teacher says, My time is at hand; I will keep the Passover at your house with my disciples.'" [19]And the disciples did as Jesus had directed them, and they prepared the Passover. [20]When it was evening, he sat at table with the twelve disciples; [21]and as they were eating, he said, "Truly, I say to you, one of you will betray me." [22]And they were very sorrowful, and began to say to him one after another, "Is it I, Lord?" [23]He answered, "He who has dipped his hand in the dish with me, will betray me. [24]The son of man goes as it is written of him, but woe to that man by whom the son of man is betrayed! It would have been better for that man if he had not

Disciple Character-Shaping Analysis #8: Matthew 26:14–25
Expanded Section: Matthew 20:17–26:29

been born." ²⁵Judas, who betrayed him, said, "Is it I, Master?" He said to him, "You have said so."

The narrator reports that Judas Iscariot goes to the chief priests and asks how much they will pay for the betrayal. It is reported that they give him thirty pieces of silver with no mention of rationale and no indication of discussion. Only this incident gives the T-CR information about the reason for Judas's betrayal. Therefore, given the payment, greed is implied as the motivation for the betrayal. The T-CR is informed that Judas accepts the payment when the narrator reports in the following sentence that Judas sought an opportunity to betray him. The T-CR thereby is clearly informed that betraying Jesus is a primary concern of Judas, and the only reason for delay is timing or opportunity. The T-CR is informed of Judas's disloyalty and greed. His motive is stated and his attitude conveyed, not by his words or actions, but by the narrator's omniscient statement of what he seeks to do.

The T-CR has been informed of the chief priests a number of times before this incident. At the time of Jesus' birth they, with the "scribes," are described by the narrator as "of the people." They demonstrate their knowledge of the prophet Micah's writings by telling Herod where the Christ is said to be born (2:3–6). This statement of the priests occurred in Jerusalem.

They are referred to again in this narrative world only when the narrator summarizes Jesus' message to the disciples, in incident five, that "he must go to Jerusalem and suffer many things from the elders, chief priests and scribes..." (16:21). The only time Jesus refers to them directly is in incident seven when he states that he goes to Jerusalem to be condemned by the chief priests and scribes (21:18). The narrator refers to them four more times, when Jesus and his followers are in Jerusalem. They are described as opponents who ask questions (21:15, 23, 45) and confer with others to arrest and kill Jesus (26:3). Thus the T-CR is clearly informed that Judas acts negatively toward Jesus when he accepts their offer. This is the first time this kind of betrayal has been reported about any of the disciples. The narrator's identification of Judas as a betrayer when he was chosen (10:4) was a gap for the T-CR which is now clarified.

After reporting Judas's preparation for betrayal, the narrator reverts to a description of the disciples as a group and their preparation for the Passover meal. The narrator reports their offer to prepare the meal and comments that they followed Jesus' instructions; they are shown as thoughtful, obedient, helpful, and respondent.

At the beginning of the meal (26:20–25), the narrator reports that the twelve disciples are present when Jesus predicts that "one of you will betray me," something the T-CR and now Jesus know about. When the disciples respond by being sorrowful, and by asking, "Is it I, Lord?" it is not clear whether they accept his prediction and are uncertain about their own intentions or that they understand that the betrayal will be unplanned or unintentional. However, the T-CR has been informed that Judas already has committed himself to this course of action and yet is not willing to admit it to Jesus and the other disciples. The eleven other disciples are not aware of Judas's cooperation with the chief priests.

Jesus (26:23–24) states that he knows that one of the twelve is a betrayer but he does not name him. Three previous times the narrator reported that Jesus understood or simply knew things that had been reported to him (9:4; 12:25; 16:8). Thus it is not unusual for the T-CR to be informed that Jesus has such knowledge. Jesus states, indirectly, that the betrayer is one of the disciples. When the narrator then reports that Judas, "who betrayed him," also asks, "Is it I, Master (*rabbi*)?" (26:25), the implication of the previous sentences for the T-CR is now clear: Judas wishes to hide his action. The addition of the descriptive phrase, "who betrayed him," makes it clear that the narrator wishes to emphasize Judas's duplicity. In addition, when Judas addresses Jesus with the title "Master" and not "Lord" as the other disciples had done (26:20), it is a clear clue for the T-CR that Judas has a lower evaluation of him.

The only time the title "Master (*rabbi*)" occurred in this narrative world was in Jesus' criticism of the scribes and Pharisees (23:5–8). He told the crowd and disciples that they should not be called "Master (*rabbi*)" like the scribes and Pharisees, because use of the title betrays a concern to be seen and appreciated by people rather than by God. Calling Jesus "Master (*rabbi*)" in 26:25 thereby indicates Judas's association with opponents. Thus the T-CR receives added information about the negative character of Judas. Judas's understanding of Jesus falls well below that of the disciples and close to that of the chief priests and Pharisees.

Jesus' final remark to Judas, "You have said so" (26:25), informs the T-CR that Jesus must know of Judas's agreement with the opponents. However, because Jesus does not provide a precise statement of what took place, this presents a gap for the T-CR. Since the T-CR knows Judas's willingness to act on behalf of the chief priests, Jesus' statement implies that he is fully aware of Judas's action and plans, even though the narrator has not reported that Jesus witnessed it or had been informed about it.

Context

The context for incident eight, following the complex view of the disciples presented in seven, is a lengthy portion of the narrative (20:29–

26:13). In addition to its length, this portion of the story does not focus on the disciples all the time. It is composed of eight narrative sections.

A. The first section (20:29–34), the healing of the two blind men, takes place as Jesus is leaving Jericho. It presents the two men as people who truly understand what Jesus can do; they have confidence in his ability to heal them. The dialogue makes it clear that Jesus agrees to do the healing, partly, at least, because of their request. The narrator reports that Jesus has "pity" on them after he hears their request. The last phrase in the section says they follow him, a term that has been used in many ways and that relates directly to the T-CR's understanding of the disciples. Thus the T-CR continues to be shown that many have followed Jesus the healer. But, whether they will follow him as the suffering Son of Man, which the disciples have been shown to miscomprehend, is not clear. The disciples are present and thus witness another example of the positive effects of Jesus' healings.

B. Two of the disciples are portrayed as obedient in the next section (21:1–11) when they go, as Jesus requests, to find the ass and colt for his entry into Jerusalem. It is important for the T-CR that the quotation from the prophet (21:5) supports the importance of their obedience. By obeying Jesus one also obeys the Father. The disciples witness the intensity of the crowd, but the narrator does not distinguish them from the crowd. Nevertheless, the crowd, quoted by the narrator, identifies Jesus as "the prophet Jesus from Nazareth of Galilee" (21:11), a positive statement but not as positive as the statements from his disciples up to this point.

C. In the next event (21:12–22) the focus shifts from the disciples to those opposed to Jesus when the narrator reports how Jesus responds to the selling activities in the temple and then, himself, heals the blind and lame. His action and the response from the children in the temple lead the chief priests and scribes to being "indignant," as stated by the narrator. Their opposition is emphasized when Jesus responds to their question about the children's positive statement. He asks them if they have never read: "Out of the mouths of babes and sucklings thou hast brought perfect praise" (21:16). No response from the opponents is reported; it is simply stated that Jesus returns to Bethany for the evening.

The second portion of this section (21:18–22) brings the disciples back into the foreground when Jesus withers the fig tree. The disciples "marveled, saying, 'How did the fig tree wither at once?'" (21:20). Jesus focuses, again, on the matter of faith: "If you have faith and never doubt, you will not only do what has been done to the fig tree, but even if you say to this mountain, 'Be taken up and cast into the sea,' it will be done" (21:21). In this statement faith is contrasted with doubt, helping to give more content to the word "faith." The disciples hear what would happen if they had faith and never doubted, and, after giving the example of moving a mountain, Jesus concludes: "And whatever you ask in prayer, you will receive, if you have faith" (21:22).

Again the importance of faith is emphasized as Jesus limits his expectations of the disciples with the conditional statement. What Jesus has done to the fig tree the disciples could do to mountains. Just as important, however, is the emphasis on prayer. In the final statement, Jesus says that faith would also give them whatever they ask in prayer. Thus for the T-CR Jesus continues to define one important attribute, faith, which he expects from the disciples. It is clear that they have not yet achieved the level of commitment that he expects, even though they have received more information about what is expected of them. They have been portrayed as people of little faith. But they continue to follow Jesus to Jerusalem and have made *some* progress in reaching Jesus' expectations. Will they continue to progress? The narrator does not report their reaction to Jesus' affirmation.

D. The next section (21:23–22:46) takes place in the temple. It is quite long. It begins when the chief priests and elders ask Jesus to explain the authority by which he does "these things." Previous actions in the temple (21:12) — driving out people who sold and bought, healing blind men — are brought to the foreground. When the chief priests and elders ask about the quality and source of his authority, Jesus responds with a question about their understanding of John the Baptist's baptism. This statement brings John the Baptist back into the foreground of the T-CR. By reporting an argument among the chief priest and elders, rather than an immediate answer, the narrator shows that they are more concerned with the response of the multitude than with answering Jesus' question, and therefore say that they "do not know" (21:27). Jesus' reply, that he will not answer their question, informs the T-CR to consider the chief priests and elders as manipulators, which Jesus has been able to demonstrate. They respond based on expectations of their answer's effect on the people, *rather* than their understanding of the question. Although the presence of disciples is not mentioned, the T-CR can add to the portrait of these opponents as distinct from, and less than, the disciples.

Jesus' conversation with the chief priests and elders continues when he asks for a judgment about a story of two sons and two responses to their father's request for labor (21:28–32). When the chief priests and elders respond that they consider the son who repents and obeys to be following the father's will, Jesus rebukes them for being *less* than tax collectors and harlots in relation to the kingdom: "You did not believe him [John the Baptist], but the tax collectors and the harlots believed him" (21:32). The T-CR thus receives further information about Jesus' criticism of the chief priests and elders. They acknowledge the importance of repentance but did not repent when asked to do so by John the

Baptist. For the T-CR one characteristic of a true follower, therefore, is the recognition of John the Baptist or Jesus as persons sent by the Father.

The narrator again reports no response to Jesus' criticism. Jesus continues to speak to the chief priests and elders (21:33–41), this time with another parable, the story of the vineyard tenants who kill the owner's servants and his son. When the chief priests and elders, in reply to Jesus' question about how the owner should react, state that the tenants should be put to death, Jesus quotes from the "scripture" with a sarcastic introduction ("Have you never read...") and explains that the kingdom of God will be taken away from them and given to a nation producing its fruits. After Jesus' conclusion, the narrator reports that the questioners wanted to arrest him, but were again afraid of the multitudes who considered Jesus a prophet. Thus the narrator informs the T-CR again of the intentions of the chief priests and elders and their rationale for rejecting Jesus' message.

Another parable follows (22:1–14), still addressed to the opponents. The parable contrasts invited guests who do not come to a marriage feast with those in the streets who receive an open invitation. A guest without the proper attire, however, is cast out — an extreme punishment. The concluding sentence is a general summation: "Many are called but few are chosen" (22:14). Thus, although the emphasis in this section clearly falls on the character of the opponents, it establishes a contrast which helps the T-CR expand his understanding of the expectations Jesus has for his followers. What Jesus wants is, in part, what the opponents are not.

This focus on the opponents continues when the narrator reports that the Pharisees reenter the scene and try to "entangle" Jesus (22:15). They send their disciples to ask a question about paying taxes to Caesar, following a polite and submissive introduction. The important phrase from the Pharisees' disciples is, "for you do not regard the position of men," a statement similar to Jesus' rebuke of Peter in chapter 16: "You are on the side of men not God." Jesus' response to their question about taxes — he calls them "hypocrites" — demonstrates his awareness of their mission to entangle him. This label, which occurs only in quotes of Jesus, has been presented more specifically as the narrative has progressed. In this instance the word connects with the idea of testing; that is, the Pharisees' disciples are reported to ask a question in order to entangle Jesus rather than to seek an answer. In the dialogue, Jesus uses the image of the coin to distinguish between what belongs to God and Caesar. The narrator reports that they marveled at the answer and departed. However, the T-CR is not informed of their thoughts or the reason for their amazement.

The opposition in the temple continues with a detailed question from the Sadducees (22:23–33). The narrator reports that they "say that there is no resurrection." Their question, however, asks Jesus' opinion about the resurrection, given a specific family situation. Jesus' reply (22:29–33) is direct: "You are wrong." Jesus says they do not understand the resurrection nor do they correctly interpret a statement by the Father. Jesus concludes with a summary statement: "He is not the God of the dead but of the living" (22:32). The narrator concludes with the crowd's, not the Sadducees', response: "They were astonished" (22:33). Again, the T-CR does not receive information about the reaction of the questioners. Nevertheless, having asked about a belief they do not accept, the Sadducees are portrayed as opponents and testers of Jesus.

In the next sentence the narrator says that the Pharisees and Sadducees come together because Jesus had silenced the Sadducees (22:34–46). Based on their work together, one of them, a lawyer, tests Jesus again: "Which is the great commandment in the law?" (22:36). Jesus' reply is straightforward: The opportunity to love God is primary, and the love of a neighbor is an important second feature; both depend on the law and the prophets, says Jesus (22:39–40).

These confrontations in the temple conclude when Jesus asks the Pharisees about the Christ: "Whose son is he?" (22:42). The Pharisees answer that the Christ is David's son. Jesus implies that their answer is invalid by quoting an inspired statement of David in which he calls the Christ "Lord." The narrator then reports, in summary form, that no one could answer Jesus' question or dare "ask him any more questions" (22:46).

In this lengthy section the chief priests, elders, Pharisees, and Sadducees are presented to the T-CR as negative characters, thus helping clarify their distinctness from the disciples. The importance of dialogue has been stressed by having a variety of opponents test Jesus. When Jesus handles all these tests in a clear, precise way, the disciples benefit indirectly in the way the T-CR understands them. Although disciples are not people with faith but people with little faith, they have progressed significantly. Following Jesus differs from testing him like the opponents.

E. The next section of the context (23:1–39) consists of a speech by Jesus, which begins with the narrator's report that Jesus addresses the crowds and his disciples. Thus the narrative shifts from Jesus' critical, questioning dialogues with opponents to Jesus' teaching about the opponents, in which his expectations and evaluations are stated directly. The subject of this teaching is stated at the beginning to be the scribes and Pharisees. Having reported the opponents' interaction with and testing of Jesus, the narrator emphasizes Jesus' negative evaluation of these opponents. The event takes place in the temple area where much of his conflict with the authorities has occurred.

Jesus begins with a description of their status: "The scribes and Pharisees sit on Moses' seat, so practice and observe whatever they tell you;

but not what they do; for they preach but do not practice" (23:3). As he has emphasized in his teaching of the disciples, one's status as a follower derives from one's recognition of and adherence to the Father's laws. Jesus refers to leaders who focus on the law but do not act in accordance with the law. Jesus then gives examples of their behavior, emphasizing that they are most interested in being seen (23:5–7). They like to be called "Master (rabbi)" and recognized for their authority. By placing too much emphasis on themselves, they have lost the required humility. Since the disciples are all brethren, says Jesus, *their* father is the heavenly Father, not their individual male parents. There is only one leader (*kathegetes*), the Christ. A summary statement ("Whoever exalts himself will be humbled, and whoever humbles himself will be exalted," 23:12) concludes this first section with the ideas of servanthood and humility.

Jesus' teaching then moves to a different format. Now he speaks to the crowds and disciples using the phrase: "But woe to you scribes and Pharisees, hypocrites!" (23:13). The T-CR has been informed of the word "woe" in two previous instances. When Jesus apparently was speaking to the crowds and not the disciples, he criticized two towns, Chorazin and Bethsaida, because they did not repent: "Woe to you" (11:21). The result, Jesus predicted, would be a negative day of judgment. Then, in the dialogue with the disciples in chapter 18, Jesus uses the same word, "woe," but this time says "woe to the *world* for temptation to sin" and "woe to the *man* by whom temptation comes" (18:7). For the T-CR, then, this word indicates Jesus' negative, critical attitude. Given the earlier negative portrayal of the scribes and Pharisees, its usage here is consistent with the narrative world. Thus the scribes and Pharisees are being judged, not addressed, and the term points to Jesus' critical attitude.

The T-CR has also received a consistent meaning for the word "hypocrite." Only Jesus uses the term in this narrative world. In his initial teaching of the disciples, Jesus used it four times: as a descriptive title for those who seek praise from *people* for performing pious actions (6:2, 5, 16), and for someone who wants to help people with problems and does not realize his own, much larger, problem (7:5). Jesus later attaches the word to the Pharisees and scribes who came to him from Jerusalem (15:1–9) and accused his disciples of not washing their hands. He criticizes them because "you have made void the word of God" (15:6). Thus when the word appears in 23:13 to categorize the scribes and Pharisees it criticizes a similar set of actions.

After the "woe" is stated Jesus explains the reason for his criticism: "because you shut the kingdom of heaven against men" (23:13). Therefore the narrator informs the T-CR in reporting a teaching of Jesus in the temple area, that Jesus criticizes opponents based on actions which he finds destructive. The crowd and disciples should not respect those who seek a positive response from humans rather than the Father.

Jesus repeats the highly critical phrase, "Woe to you scribes and Pharisees, hypocrites!" five more times. Once he says, "Woe to you, blind guides" (23:16). Their actions are described as unacceptable for the pious people they claim to be. They mistreat and work against people they convert; they emphasize gold rather than the temple as the presence of God; they request the tithing of one's possessions; and they are unwilling to recognize their limitations. They are described as using misguided action to lead people astray. They lack perception of the Father's concerns, especially "law, justice and mercy and faith" (23:23); they are "full of hypocrisy and iniquity" (23:28).

Because of this description, Jesus says he will send "prophets, wise men and scribes" whom the scribes and Pharisees will attack, persecute, and kill. Scribes and Pharisees will act consistent with their present practice of performing deeds they claim are in line with God's demands, but which clearly are not. Thus the T-CR is informed, in a new way, of Jesus' expectation of the disciples by seeing in detail why Jesus denounces the hypocrites.

This address concludes with continued emphasis on the persecution of God's messengers. The words are addressed to the city of the Pharisees and scribes, Jerusalem. Using the metaphor of a hen gathering her brood, Jesus condemns the persecution in the city. Jesus concludes with a threat: "You will not see me again until you say, 'Blessed is he who comes in the name of the Lord'" (23:39). Thus his criticism of the Pharisees and scribes warns the disciples about the reception they can expect. The city is characterized as insensitive to the prophets and those who come from the Lord. Therefore the T-CR sees again that Jesus anticipates his fate, that he warns the disciples, and that his opponents cause his problems.

F. The sixth section (24:1–25:46) of the context begins with the report that Jesus leaves the temple and that the disciples "point out to him the buildings of the temple." No reason is given for the disciples' action, but Jesus implies that they express positive feelings for the temple. Jesus replies by predicting its destruction, something the T-CR can understand given the many instances in this context in which the temple has been a place of conflict and controversy. The narrator does not report the reaction of the disciples until they reach the Mount of Olives, where they ask Jesus when the destruction will take place and state their understanding that it will mark Jesus' coming and the close of the age (24:3).

Jesus' reply to the disciples begins with a warning about being deceived by false messiahs, by the rumors of wars, and by earthquakes and famines. Such events are just the beginning. The real issue, says Jesus, is

that the disciples will be persecuted and killed (24:9). The coming of
the end will cause various types of trouble, but those who endure to
the end will be saved. He states that the gospel of the kingdom will be
preached before the end will come. Thus although the disciples are not
named specifically as the preachers of the kingdom, they are warned
of the troubles that will precede the end time. As followers of Jesus
they should anticipate real difficulties. Thus the T-CR receives more information about Jesus' expectations of the disciples than about their
character.

Then his advice becomes more specific. He tells the disciples to flee
once the end is approaching (24:15–19). There can be no delay or
uncertainty. The primary concern that Jesus has, in speaking to the disciples, is that they could be misled by the false messiahs or prophets
(24:24). The image that he uses as a sign of correct understanding
is lightning. The coming of the Son of Man will be as obvious as
lightning to anyone who is aware (24:27). Another image forms the
conclusion to this section. Wherever the body is, there the eagles will
gather. The narrator does not interrupt Jesus' speech to indicate what
effect it has on the disciples. The important aspect for the T-CR is
that Jesus now informs the disciples of the drastic implications of his
presence, in contrast to his earlier emphasis on expectations of their
"following" action.

Jesus' stress on the future continues (24:29–31) with predictions
about changes in the universe beyond the difficult times facing people
on earth. The coming of the Son of Man will be accompanied by extensive changes in the heavens, the area of the universe controlled by
the Father. The coming of the Son of Man will then be obvious, and
the elect will fully recognize it. Thus the disciples are encouraged to live
through the difficulties because of the positive results to come.

The use of metaphor continues with the statement that summer is
near when the fig tree puts forth its leaves (24:32). Similarly one will
know the Son of Man has come when the previously stated events take
place (24:33). Jesus says that the current generation will experience the
things to which he refers. What will not be lost, even with the drastic
changes in the universe, are "my words" (24:35). Since the teaching
of Jesus assumes the utmost importance in this narrative world, the
T-CR has no difficulty understanding this claim. But, since the disciples
have not been able to understand and accept Jesus' message and its requirements, there remains some question for the T-CR about how the
disciples will respond.

It is even more significant that, in the next part of the speech (24:36–
44), Jesus indicates that he does not know the hour when these events
will take place. The reference to people saved from the flood, or to
people who disappear in time of tribulation, indicates that the earth's

inhabitants do not know the timing of the Father's actions. Jesus says that one must "watch." The use of metaphor continues with the story of the householder who does not know when the thief is coming. As the householder must be ready, so the disciples must stay alert for the world-shaking arrival of the son.

There is then, in the following story of the faithful slave, a shift toward a positive image (24:45–51). Although Jesus does not call the story a parable, it presents to the disciples a picture of the activity Jesus expects from them. The servant who acts as his master requires will be rewarded when the master returns. But, if he acts contemptibly, the servant will be punished, or "put with the hypocrites" (24:51). For the T-CR, mention of the hypocrites, who were clearly defined in the final speech in the temple (23:1–39), emphasizes the heavy criticism of the scribes and Pharisees and possibly shows a positive attitude toward the disciples. Since this section ends with the statement, "there men will weep and gnash their teeth," the T-CR also is informed of Jesus' emphasis upon the fate of those who do not respond to the Father's message.

Having mentioned earlier the importance of preaching the gospel of the kingdom, Jesus now uses another metaphor, stating that "the kingdom of heaven shall be compared to ten maidens who took their lamps and went to meet the bridegroom" (25:1). Jesus, in his response to the disciples' question about the sign of the coming age, had focused previously on the troubles to be expected and had offered metaphors to illustrate the expectations he has for them. Now Jesus has switched to a specific parable, like the parables in chapter 13, which the disciples claimed they could comprehend — though they had not always comprehended Jesus' metaphoric teaching. This parable (25:1–13) compares those who are prepared and those who are not. When the five foolish maidens arrive late to the marriage feast, due to their lack of preparation, they are not permitted to enter. Jesus' concluding statement informs the disciples of the main point: "Watch therefore, for you know neither the day nor the hour" (25:13). As stated earlier, "watch" implies being fully prepared for the end, not merely the passive sense of looking forward to it. Therefore the T-CR is informed of Jesus' opinion that certain actions and responsibilities are required of any followers who hope to survive at the end and receive acceptance from the Lord.

The same point is stressed in the next parable (25:14–30) although it begins differently: "For it will be as when a man going on a journey...." This story concentrates on three servants and the money they receive to use for the master's benefit while he is away. Those who use successfully the amount they receive are called "good and faithful" because they have been "faithful over a little" (25:21). The servant who is not faithful says he was afraid. Thus the master in this parable expects support and recognition of his requirement that servants work on his behalf with what they have been given. The T-CR is being informed that fear of work during a master's absence is a problem that the disciples should anticipate. The story ends with a previously employed reference to the outer darkness: "There men will weep and gnash their teeth" (25:30).

The next story begins with a reference to the Son of Man (25:31), describing him on his throne, judging all the nations. Those who receive a positive response from him, "the sheep," have acted in a way that he admires, though they did not know that they were responding to his needs. The opposite group, "the goats," claim they did not see him and were not required to help him. Being a true follower means performing actions on behalf of people in need; it is the proper way to "watch." The righteous act in a way judged positively by the king, because they have helped his people. The conclusion informs the T-CR of the parable's interpretation, that the evil go "into eternal punishment," the righteous "into eternal life."

The T-CR is informed more about Jesus' expectations in this lengthy teaching, especially regarding the relationship between his death and resurrection and the subsequent coming of the kingdom. Now that he approaches his suffering, death, and resurrection, he stresses his action beyond these major events. The approach of the kingdom, the reason for repentance, is immediate.

Finally, the flow of the story changes with the report that, when Jesus finished these sayings, he spoke to the disciples: "You know that after two days the Passover is coming, and the Son of Man will be delivered up to be crucified" (26:2). Thus the T-CR is informed that after a lengthy dialogue about the difficulties of the immediate and extended future, Jesus wants to keep the disciples' attention focused on the reason he came to Jerusalem and on his confirmation with the hypocrites. This is the sixth time the T-CR has learned about Jesus' fate, but it is the first time a precise connection between the Passover and the crucifixion appears.

G. The context continues (26:3–5) in the narrator's report that the chief priests and elders have gathered to plot Jesus' arrest and to kill him. Thus the T-CR sees that Jesus' prediction corresponds with the opponents' intention. The disciples are not aware of the coming arrest, but the T-CR is informed that they should recognize the reality of Jesus' statements about his suffering and death. However, the opponents will not act immediately because, the narrator reports, they once again do not want to cause "tumult" among the people. Thus, conditions now exist for actions that could lead to the death of Jesus, as he has predicted.

Immediate Context

The incident (26:6–13) preceding character-shaping incident eight begins with a shift of location from Jerusalem to Bethany. While Jesus eats with "Simon, the leper," showing his concern for the unhealthy and "sinners" (9:10–13), a woman anoints his head with expensive ointment. The narrator describes the disciples as indignant, and they wish to sell the ointment and give "the large sum" to the poor. Thus, their reaction shows the T-CR that they indeed have learned something from the teaching of Jesus. However, Jesus does not approve of the disciples' indignation. His response has to do with timing: the woman has performed an acceptable act because Jesus interprets it as a preparation for burial. As a result, she will be remembered. The disciples again have been criticized for not recognizing the importance of the time in which they live, the days just prior to Jesus' death and resurrection.

The T-CR had been informed a few sentences before about Jesus' prediction of his death (26:2) and the planned arrest and crucifixion by the chief priests, elders, and high priests. The information the T-CR receives emphasizes the importance of the moment. The death of Jesus is imminent, and, therefore, affects how actions will be evaluated. The disciples' inadequacy, while not extreme, calls their attention to what the T-CR already knows — that the end of Jesus' life is at hand. At the same time, the T-CR anticipates a situation in which opponents can arrest Jesus without violating their concern for the reaction of the people. Thus Jesus criticizes the disciples, in spite of their concern for the poor, both for "troubling the woman" (26:10) and for not being aware of his coming fate (26:12).

Summary

The context for this incident provides the longest portion of Matthew's gospel without a disciple character-shaping incident. However, the material prepares the T-CR for Judas's betrayal and presents significant information affecting the portrayal of the disciples.

The context prepares the T-CR for Judas's action by focusing on Jerusalem and the temple, where Jesus demonstrates his antagonism toward the chief priests, elders, Pharisees, and Sadducees. By not mentioning the disciples, the narrator stresses to the T-CR the importance of the opponents' character and intensity. With questioning from the opponents complete, Jesus criticizes them before the crowds and the disciples, labeling them hypocrites (23:1–39). After elaborating his criticism, he responds at length to the disciples' question about the need to "watch" because of the importance of certain future events (24:1–

25:46). He concludes the dialogue with parables, an aspect of Jesus' teaching that the T-CR knows the disciples have a limited ability to comprehend. Then, in preparation for the incident involving Judas, the T-CR hears Jesus' interpretation of his anointing by the woman (26:6–13). Although the T-CR does not learn the reasons for the woman's action, Jesus makes it clear in responding to the disciples' objection that it is an appropriate preparation for his death.

The T-CR has received, here and throughout the narrative, large amounts of information about Jesus' expectations of the disciples. As the story progresses, the T-CR sees that the disciples are not meeting those requirements though they continue to follow him and, at times, act positively. They have *little* faith, but are not *without* faith. In addition, the emphasis continues on Jesus' opponents, giving the T-CR a clearer distinction between the opponents and the disciples.

However, Judas, one of the twelve disciples, cooperates with the opponents in this incident and tries to help them take Jesus' life with minimal crowd reaction. With the focus on Judas the "betrayer," who acts in accordance with the narrator's earlier statement about him, the inevitability of Jesus' death now becomes comprehensible for the T-CR. In addition, since this incident begins with the word "then" (*tote*), the T-CR is informed that Judas in some sense is responding to Jesus' criticism of the disciples (26:10–13), who had complained about Jesus' anointment. That Judas agrees to work with the opponents for thirty silver pieces, after being criticized for objecting to the woman's use of the ointment, gives the T-CR added information about his action. Judas appears more concerned with the acquisition of funds, and how they will be used, than with the status, significance, and fate of Jesus. Judas does not act as a representative of the followers but apparently acts on his own. The response that helps define his character is his unwavering acceptance of the silver that the opponents offer.

By describing a disciple who acts on his own, independent from other followers, this incident differs from other portrayals of the disciples in this narrative world. Judas's rationale is not clear, other than the apparent emphasis upon money. But Jesus' death now appears a more likely occurrence, a disciple having agreed to work with his opponents. The negativity of the portrayal of a disciple, based on his agreement with the opponents, is a gap for the T-CR about whether the other disciples will also become non-followers.

Character-Shaping Incident Nine:

PETER'S DENIAL
Matt. 26:30–58, [59–68], 69–75

BECAUSE THIS character-shaping incident is 46 verses, and the preceding context section is only five verses, the incident itself covers most of the expanded section on the chart. The chart also demonstrates that dialogue and disciple response are the predominant characteristics of this character-shaping incident. As is evident on the lower, full-story section of the chart, this is the last incident in which dialogue and teaching form important contexts for the disciples' response. Because of the intense interaction between Jesus and the disciples, the portrait of the disciples becomes much more explicit.

Details of Event

This long section focuses on Peter, who is presented to the T-CR both as an individual and as a representative of the disciples. After claiming they will not deny him, Peter, James, and John disobey Jesus' command to stay awake when accompanying him in his sorrow. The arrest occurs when Judas brings the crowd of opponents. The eleven disciples flee — but then Peter follows Jesus, at a distance, to the courtyard as a stranger. He denies any connection to Jesus, as Jesus had predicted.

³⁰And when they had sung a hymn, they went out to the Mount of Olives. ³¹Then Jesus said to them, "You will all fall away because of me this night; for it is written, 'I will strike the shepherd, and the sheep of the flock will be scattered.' ³²But after I am raised up, I will go before you to Galilee." ³³Peter declared to him, "Though they all fall away because of you, I will never fall away." ³⁴Jesus said to him, "Truly, I say to you, this very night, before the cock crows, you will deny me three times." ³⁵Peter said to him, "Even if I must die with you, I will not deny you." And so said all the disciples.

³⁶Then Jesus went with them to a place called Gethsemane, and he said to his disciples, "Sit here, while I go yonder and pray." ³⁷And

taking with him Peter and the two sons of Zebedee, he began to be sorrowful and troubled. [38]Then he said to them, "My soul is very sorrowful, even to death; remain here, and watch with me." [39]And going a little farther he fell on his face and prayed, "My Father, if it be possible, let this cup pass from me; nevertheless, not as I will, but as thou wilt." [40]And he came to the disciples and found them sleeping; and he said to Peter, "So, could you not watch with me one hour? [41]Watch and pray that you may not enter into temptation; the spirit indeed is willing, but the flesh is weak." [42]Again, for the second time, he went away and prayed, "My Father, if this cannot pass unless I drink it, thy will be done." [43]And again he came and found them sleeping, for their eyes were heavy. [44]So, leaving them again, he went away and prayed for the third time, saying the same words. [45]Then he came to the disciples and said to them, "Are you still sleeping and taking your rest? Behold the hour is at hand, and the Son of Man is betrayed into the hands of sinners. [46]Rise, let us be going; see, my betrayer is at hand."

[47]While he was still speaking, Judas came, one of the twelve, and with him a great crowd with swords and clubs, from the chief priests and the elders of the people. [48]Now the betrayer had given them a sign, saying, "The one I shall kiss is the man; seize him." [49]And he came up to Jesus at once and said, "Hail, Master!" And he kissed him. [50]Jesus said to him, "Friend, why are you here?" Then they came up and laid hands on Jesus and seized him. [51]And behold, one of those who were with Jesus stretched out his hand and drew his sword, and struck the slave of the high priest, and cut off his ear. [52]Then Jesus said to him, "Put your sword back into its place; for all who take the sword will perish by the sword. [53]Do you think that I cannot appeal to my Father, and he will at once send me more than twelve legions of angels? [54]But how then should the scriptures be fulfilled, that it must be so?" [55]At that hour Jesus said to the crowds, "Have you come as against a robber, with swords and clubs to capture me? Day after day I sat in the temple teaching, and you did not seize me. [56]But all this has taken place, that the scriptures of the prophets might be fulfilled." Then all the disciples forsook him and fled.

[57]Then those who had seized Jesus led him to Caiaphas the high priest, where the scribes and the elders had gathered. [58]But Peter followed him at a distance, as far as the courtyard of the high priest, and going inside he sat with the guards to see the end. [[59]Now the chief priests and the whole council sought false testimony against Jesus that they might put him to death, [60]but they found none, though many false witnesses came forward. At last

Disciple Character-Shaping Analysis #9: Matthew 26:30–75
Expanded Section: Matthew 26:26–27:2

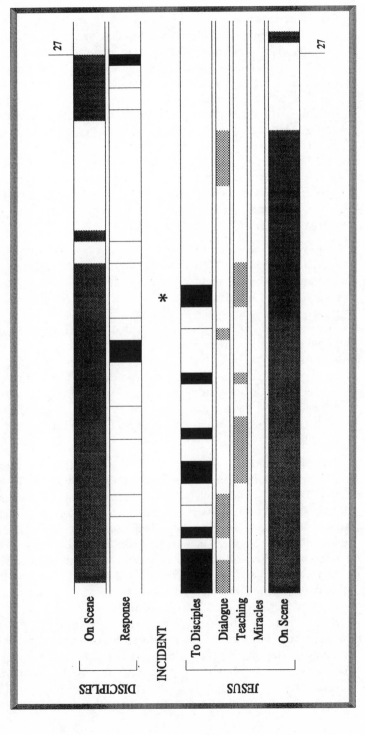

two came forward [61]and said, "This fellow said, 'I am able to destroy the temple of God, and to build it in three days.' " [62]And the high priest stood up and said, "Have you no answer to make? What is it that these men testify against you?" [63]But Jesus was silent. And the high priest said to him, "I adjure you by the living God, tell us if you are the Christ, the Son of God." [64]Jesus said to him, "You have said so. But I tell you, hereafter you will see the Son of Man seated at the right hand of Power, and coming on the clouds of heaven." [65]Then the high priest tore his robes, and said, "He has uttered blasphemy. Why do we still need witnesses? You have now heard his blasphemy. [66]What is your judgment?" They answered, "He deserves death." [67]Then they spat in his face, and struck him; and some slapped him, [68]saying, "Prophesy to us, you Christ! Who is it that struck you?"]

[69]Now Peter was sitting outside in the courtyard. And a maid came up to him, and said, "You also were with Jesus the Galilean." [70]But he denied it before them all, saying, "I do not know what you mean." [71]And when he went out to the porch, another maid saw him, and she said to the bystanders, "This man was with Jesus of Nazareth." [72]And again he denied it with an oath, "I do not know the man." [73]After a little while the bystanders came up and said to Peter, "Certainly you are also one of them, for your accent betrays you." [74]Then he began to invoke a curse on himself and to swear, "I do not know the man." And immediately the cock crowed. [75]And Peter remembered the saying of Jesus, "Before the cock crows, you will deny me three times." And he went out and wept bitterly.

This is an important incident for the T-CR because it develops Jesus' confrontation both with his opponents and followers. After Jesus predicts that the disciples will fall away that night, yet survive the crisis (26:31–32), Peter again asserts his intent to maintain Jesus' high expectations. When Jesus reaffirms his prediction, Peter says he is willing to "die with you" (26:35). The narrator adds that all the disciples say the same thing. Thus the T-CR is clearly presented with the disciples as followers who recognize the life-threatening danger of following the Son of Man. They claim that they are willing to go to their death. Thus they seem to be aware of what Jesus asks of them.

Rather than reporting Jesus' evaluation of their devotion, the narrator states that Jesus goes with the disciples to Gethsemane. Asking the disciples to stay in one place, Jesus takes Peter, James, and John to a more private location. These are the three reported to have seen Jesus' transfiguration and whom the Father told to listen to Jesus (17:5). Significantly for the T-CR, the *narrator* reports that Jesus is sorrowful and troubled (26:38), and then quotes Jesus mentioning his sorrow to the disciples and asking them to "watch" (or be awake, 26:38). The disciples had been told previously to watch when preparing for the "day your Lord is coming" (24:42). Jesus had used the word "watch" three times in the previous teaching to the disciples; for the T-CR the word forms part of Jesus' expectations: "Watch, therefore, for you do not know on what day your Lord is coming" (24:42); "But know this, that if the householder had known in what part of the night the thief was coming, he would have watched and would not have let his house be broken into" (24:43); "Watch therefore, for you know neither the day nor the hour" (25:13). Jesus thus informs the disciples of the importance of this moment.

After praying to the Father, whereby the T-CR is informed of the depth of Jesus' sorrow, he returns to the three disciples and finds them sleeping. His statement to Peter reaffirms the importance of watching. He tells the disciples, "Watch and pray that you may not enter into temptation" (26:41). But after reporting another of Jesus' prayers — about the Father's will — the narrator says the disciples cannot maintain the watch. They sleep because their eyes are heavy (26:43). Jesus' final response to their sleeping (not watching), following his third prayer, no longer conveys expectation. He states that the crisis that he had predicted, which the disciples said they could endure, has arrived (26:46). Thus the disciples' limited qualifications, especially their inability to watch, are portrayed clearly.

The narrator states that Judas fulfills the agreement he had with the authorities by identifying Jesus (26:49). Again he calls Jesus "Master (*rabbi*)," informing the T-CR that his understanding of Jesus has not changed since using the term after his initial cooperation with the opponents (26:25). The narrator flashes back to an earlier arrangement with opponents (26:48) to explain why Judas identifies Jesus with a kiss. The statements about Judas as the betrayer are thus confirmed. Judas's intention is complete.

Jesus responds by saying, "Friend, why are you here?" (26:50). Jesus had used the word "friend" twice, in two metaphorical stories, in which the main figure addressed a person who complained (20:13) or who had acted unacceptably. Thus the T-CR is informed that Jesus recognizes what Judas had done, but the narrator does not report that Judas responds. Though Jesus knew that Judas would come and betray him, this incident serves to confirm Jesus' (and the T-CR's) awareness of the impending arrest.

When Jesus is seized, an unidentified follower is reported to cut off the ear of a slave of the high priest (26:51). Jesus calls use of the sword inappropriate, having predicted resistance against his capture and that it would be understandable despite the disciples' stated willingness to die. But Jesus reaffirms his intent to follow the Father's guidelines, as stated in his prayers. Therefore, resistance is unnecessary. Jesus' rhetorical questions (26:53–54) inform the T-CR that, in his opinion, the disciples should have understood the situation.

The narrator reports that the "crowd" which accompanies Judas is a select group to help Judas in his betrayal: " ... and with him a great crowd with swords and clubs, from the chief priests and elders of the people" (26:47). Jesus then asks the crowd about their action, referring to an earlier time in the temple when he was not "seized" by them (26:55). Jesus thus points the T-CR to authorities' earlier concern to capture Jesus when the crowd would not be upset. His final statement refers to the incident as a fulfillment of the prophets, but there is no quotation from the prophets (26:56). For the T-CR, Jesus indicates his primary objective to follow the will of the Father. By appealing to the fulfillment of scripture (26:54), while not citing the text, Jesus emphasizes the narrator's use of fulfillment quotations to demonstrate the close relationship between Jesus and the Father. The fulfillment of scripture had been stated clearly in the framework of the narrative as a sign of their kinship.

The narrator's next comment, then, has added significance: "Then all the disciples forsook him and fled" (26:56). Despite their statements that they would follow Jesus, even to his death, and despite a desire to fulfill the will of the Father, they nevertheless do not want to be arrested. Thus their action demonstrates no connection with their previous assertions. The way they act now is not how they said they *would* act. This portrayal of the disciples, connected to their promise in 26:35 to stay with Jesus, shows the T-CR they are incapable of acting as promised. Initially commanded to follow Jesus, they now have fled. The arrest was even carried out with the help of a disciple. Their actions, as a way of understanding their character, show the T-CR that they fail to meet Jesus' expectations and do not measure up to their own statements of willingness to follow.

As Jesus is led away, the narrator informs the T-CR that Peter, a dedicated disciple who nevertheless fled at the arrest, does follow at a distance, erasing for the T-CR some of the negative connotations. He is at least willing to sit with the guards "to see the end" (26:58).

At this point, the narrator reports that the chief priests and council look for a way at the trial to put Jesus to death (26:59). Jesus is silent when asked to respond to two witnesses described as false, showing the T-CR the deception of his opponents. Jesus does speak in response to the command from the high priest to describe his status in relation to the Father. He emphasizes neither the past nor the present, but the future, when the Son of Man comes in power. Thus, Jesus explains, his status is not confirmed in the present by testimony on his behalf, but by the Father in the future. This reply brings condemnation and physical abuse from the council (26:66–68).

The narrator returns to Peter, having reported to the T-CR the action of the council. Peter denies three times, when confronted by maids and a bystander, that he is connected with Jesus and his followers. At first he says he does not know what their statements mean. But then with an oath and, finally, invoking "a curse on himself," he says: "I do not know the man" (26:69–74). When the narrator reports that the cock crows, he adds that Peter remembers Jesus' words about denial and that Peter "went out and wept bitterly" (26:75).

This reaction informs the T-CR that Peter realizes that he has acted contrary to his previous claim. He is now aware of his limitations and the accuracy of Jesus' prediction. Peter as an individual appears in this incident as distinct from the disciples. Though he follows Jesus to the courtyard, he is there, according to the narrator, "to see the end" (26:58). Both Peter and the other disciples are unwilling to accept the responsibility and implications of following Jesus that they had earlier affirmed. Jesus, on the other hand, demonstrates his consistent character — his willingness to accept any implication of following his Father.

The portrayal of the disciples in this incident is indeed complex. Judas carries out his agreement with Jesus' opponents, finding a time when the arrest would avoid objections from the crowd. Peter, James and John are unable to stay awake and "watch" on behalf of Jesus after following him to a private area of Gethsemane. The eleven disciples act similarly when Jesus is captured: They "forsook him and fled." Although Peter then follows Jesus "at a distance," when challenged to acknowledge his relationship to Jesus, he denies it. The T-CR sees Peter "follow" Jesus, but only to observe the trial, not to support him or become a witness. Thus the T-CR receives the most negative portrayal of the disciples to this point.

Immediate Context

Since only one incident (26:26–29) falls between character-shaping incident nine and incident eight, the only context is the *immediate* context. Because incident eight occurs just a few verses earlier than nine, it is, for the T-CR, important in setting the stage.

After Judas appears in incident eight, not admitting his intention to betray Jesus, the narrator describes Jesus' distribution of bread and wine, which Jesus identifies as his body and blood. Thus the T-CR is informed of Jesus' own interpretation of the coming crisis, and that it is likely to take place soon because of the intentions of Judas. At the same time, Jesus says the crisis occurs for the forgiveness of sins. "For this is my blood of the covenant, which is poured out for many for the forgiveness of sins" (26:28). Following the emphasis on his death, Jesus puts the event into the context of the future: "I tell you I shall not drink again of this fruit of the vine until that day when I drink it new with you in my Father's kingdom" (26:29). The T-CR is informed that, according to Jesus, a limited follower can still enter the Father's kingdom; that is, a follower's sins will be forgiven. Although failing to meet his expectations, the follower can anticipate a positive future after death. There is no indication that the disciples respond to Jesus' statement, though they continue to follow him to the Mount of Olives (26:30).

Therefore, the immediate context helps the T-CR understand Jesus' acceptance of his betrayal and death. It also helps the T-CR understand Jesus' recognition of the disciples' limitations, but shows Jesus, in pouring out his blood in forgiveness, assuring their presence in the kingdom (26:28). The continued emphasis on the death of Jesus, of which the disciples are fully informed, sets the stage for Peter's confident assertion of loyalty, which the character-shaping incident to follow shows he does not achieve.

Summary

The T-CR has been informed many times about the expectation of Jesus' trial and condemnation, and, in incident eight, learns of Judas's willingness to turn Jesus over to the chief priests and elders. When the short context focuses on Jesus telling the disciples about the significance of his death — "for the forgiveness of sins" (26:28) — and about the coming of the Father's kingdom, the disciples continue to be portrayed as recipients of Jesus' important claim to status as the son of the Father.

As the incident develops, Peter appears as a disciple who has understood the importance of Jesus' death. But Jesus predicts that Peter will not stay loyal. After the three disciples who had witnessed Jesus' transfiguration fall asleep when Jesus converses with his Father, Judas betrays him, fulfilling his role as an unusual disciple who supports the opponents. The disciples, unable to stop Jesus' arrest, flee. The T-CR thereby receives the most negative portrayal of the disciples in the narrative world. The disciples are seen as followers who will not put themselves in a dangerous situation despite their promise *never* to deny Jesus (26:35).

The focus on Peter continues as he follows Jesus and the opponents to Jesus' trial. Most important, he is unable to admit to two individuals and bystanders that he is one of Jesus' followers. Thus the T-CR continues to receive the same information about Peter. He is portrayed as a responsive and determined follower who nevertheless possesses little faith. As with the other disciples, he cannot fulfill Jesus' expectations.

The disciples, though less than ideal, had not been portrayed previously as *un*qualified followers, except for the betrayer Judas. They had continued to follow Jesus and, at times, had shown positive signs of learning Jesus' expectations and some of his teaching. Except for Judas, they differed from the opponents.

But, in this incident, the T-CR receives an extremely negative characterization. In a sense, Jesus' recognition of their "little faith" has been verified. Despite their attempts to be acceptable followers, they have not understood what it means to be a "fisher of people," though Jesus has tried to teach them. They have been taught, and have listened, but have not comprehended. The negative portrayal only increases when they flee during Jesus' arrest.

JUDAS ISCARIOT REPENTS
AND COMMITS SUICIDE
Matt. 27:3–10

O NLY TWO VERSES separate incident ten from the previous incident. The expanded chart, which displays only a small section
of chapter 27, demonstrates that the disciples react to events
that other characters besides Jesus initiated. It is also clear that Jesus'
dialogue, which takes place later, is not directed to the disciples. They
are not "on scene" at that point in the story.

Details of Event

The incident records Judas's change of mind, regret, and suicide when
he hears of Jesus' condemnation. It also records the reaction of the chief
priests and elders when Judas returns the silver.

> [3]When Judas, his betrayer, saw that he was condemned, he re-
> pented and brought back the thirty pieces of silver to the chief
> priests and elders, [4]saying, "I have sinned in betraying innocent
> blood." They said, "What is that to us? See to it yourself." [5]And
> throwing down the pieces of silver in the temple, he departed;
> and he went and hanged himself. [6]But the chief priests, taking the
> pieces of silver, said, "It is not lawful to put them into the treasury,
> since they are blood money." [7]So they took counsel, and bought
> with them the potter's field, to bury strangers in. [8]Therefore that
> field has been called the Field of Blood to this day. [9]Then was ful-
> filled what had been spoken by the prophet Jeremiah, saying, "And
> they took the thirty pieces of silver, the price of him on whom a
> price had been set by some of the sons of Israel, [10]and they gave
> them for the potter's field, as the Lord directed me."

The narrator reports that Judas repented when he saw that Jesus
was condemned (27:3). Because the purpose of his betrayal was only
implied, the T-CR still is not informed. Nevertheless, Judas has, for some

Disciple Character-Shaping Analysis #10: Matthew 27:3–10
Expanded Section: Matthew 27:1–14

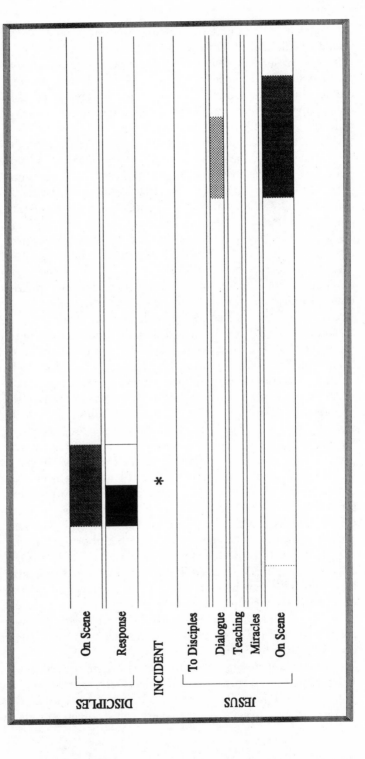

reason, changed his mind, showing the T-CR he did not expect that Jesus would be condemned. Only Jesus has used the word "repent' previously. While addressing the chief priests and elders, Jesus describes a repenter as someone who changes from a negative to a positive response (21:29). He concludes by accusing the opponents of having not changed their understanding of John the Baptist: "You did not afterward repent and believe him" (21:32).

Thus the T-CR is informed that Judas does change his mind, which is why he returns thirty pieces of silver and commits suicide. Judas is portrayed as a betrayer, but also as one who later recognizes the impropriety of his cooperation with Jesus' opponents. Demonstrating the reality of Judas's repentance, the narrator reports that Judas first returns the thirty pieces of silver, the money he received for revealing where Jesus could be arrested without raising the ire of the crowd. The narrator quotes Judas: "I have sinned in betraying innocent blood" (27:4). Thus the T-CR is given detailed information about a character's response to an event, but still does not know his initial purpose: Judas admits the innocence of Jesus, yet the T-CR is still not informed of Judas's original intent as a betrayer. Since Jesus' condemnation appears to cause Judas's repentance, the T-CR is informed that Judas apparently did not expect this result. Or once it occurs, Judas realizes the negative consequences of his action. The T-CR is informed only of Judas's action and later repentance. His purpose as a betrayer is a definite gap in this narrative world. What he thought his action would accomplish is not revealed.

The chief priests and elders respond to Judas's confession of sin by showing no concern for his guilt. They place responsibility on Judas: "What is that to us? See to it yourself" (27:4). The narrator then reports with concise precision that Judas throws down the pieces of silver in the temple and hangs himself (27:5). Thus the action of Judas demonstrates the reality of his self-image as a sinner. Although he destroys himself because of his cooperation with opponents, no specific reason is provided to explain the purpose of his betrayal. The narrator's report that Jesus is condemned by the Jewish authorities informs the T-CR that Jesus' predictions of his fate (16:21; 17:22–23; 21:18–19, 28; 26:2, 12) are becoming real possibilities. Jesus has stated a number of times that he would soon be killed. The T-CR has received limited information about Judas's purpose in arranging for Jesus' arrest; whatever his rationale, he did not expect Jesus to be condemned. In this portion of the portrayal of Judas, the emphasis is on his action and repentance, not on his reasons for betrayal.

Although not stating whether the chief priests and elders are aware of Judas's suicide, the narrator quotes their realization that the money had brought about Jesus' condemnation ("blood money," 27:6) and their decision to buy a field as a cemetery for strangers. At this point the narrator reports the result of their action, one of the few times this format appears: "Therefore that field has been called the Field of Blood to this day" (27:8).

The incident concludes with a fulfillment quotation from the prophet Jeremiah (27:9–10). The saying refers to thirty pieces of silver used to purchase a potter's field. Thus the narrator impresses upon the T-CR the significance of Jesus' betrayal. All the fulfillment quotations have underlined the connection between events in the narrative and the will of the Father. The Father has obviously not caused every event in this narrative world, but has been responsible for many incidents in the story which are related to his son. The Father does exert control over many aspects of Jesus' career. Thus, this fulfillment quotation informs the T-CR that Judas's betrayal and his recognition of guilt are consistent with the overall plan and purpose of the Father, within the narrative of the life of Jesus.

Immediate Context

There are only two verses (27:1–2) — one sentence — between Peter's denial and Judas's betrayal (character-shaping incident nine) and the story of Judas's repentance and suicide (incident ten).

The narrator uses a short statement to inform the T-CR about the results of Jesus' trial before the Sanhedrin. It begins by establishing the time (morning), an allusion to the crowing of the cock, which Peter has just heard. All the chief priests and elders "took counsel" against Jesus to decide to put him to death. Thus the decision mentioned in 26:66 ("They answered, 'He deserves death'") is restated. That they deliver Jesus to "Pilate the governor" suggests an underlying reason for the action, but the narrator does not mention it; the absence of explanation is another gap for the T-CR. Since the narrator mentions that Jesus is bound and delivered to Pilate before Judas's repentance and suicide, the T-CR is informed that Judas either watches Jesus being led away or hears of the action from Jewish authorities. The first section of the report also informs the T-CR by noting that Judas "saw that he was condemned" (27:3).

The immediate context is crucial in understanding the term "condemned." As indicated in the text of the incident, the T-CR does not know Judas's purpose in betraying Jesus. This short context does not help the T-CR fill that gap. Judging from his remorse and suicide, Judas, through his betrayal, *may* not have intended to bring about Jesus' death. He might have had a less drastic intent. However, since Jesus had predicted that his fate would be imposed by the Jewish authorities, one possible implication is that Judas did not take Jesus seriously. Because

of the gaps in this narrative world, Judas is portrayed in only limited
fashion, as one who betrays Jesus and helps bring about Jesus' condemnation, but also, perhaps, as a disciple who did not understand that his
betrayal would have such drastic effects. His suicide informs the T-CR
of his regret for his role in Jesus' condemnation.

Summary

This incident does not greatly affect the T-CR's understanding of the disciples as a group. It certainly adds complexity to the characterization of
Judas, but contains significant gaps that prevent the T-CR from gaining
information about the rationale behind his actions. He is clearly the betrayer, as previously identified (10:4), but there is no reason stated for
his betrayal, repentance, or suicide. With the characterization incomplete, the T-CR can see the portentousness of Judas's action, but also
that he is portrayed differently from the rest of the disciples. At his death
he is no longer an active character in the narrative.

The T-CR is informed of the activity of the Sanhedrin, the opponents,
setting the stage for Jesus' death and resurrection. Jesus, in being delivered to Pilate, continues in the direction he said he would be required
to move. One disciple has betrayed him by being directly involved in
Jesus' capture by the chief priests and elders and has committed suicide
after realizing the intention and action of the opponents. The other ten
disciples have fled. They are not mentioned as having heard about or
having responded to Jesus' fate. Peter has shown interest in Jesus' trial
and fate, but was unwilling to acknowledge his association with the Son
of Man. The T-CR has received an almost totally negative portrayal of
the disciples.

The T-CR, then, by this point in the story has received detailed information which underlines the truth of Jesus' description of the disciples
as people of "little faith." They have demonstrated how small their faith
is. Their concern to avoid condemnation from others, especially from
the chief priests, elders, Pharisees, and Sadducees, is apparently more
important to them than their relationship with the Father. They seem to
act like hypocrites, whom Jesus had condemned in teaching the crowds
and disciples (23:2–39). Hypocrites act for their advantage and show
little concern for others. The number of supporters or followers of Jesus
appears to have fallen to zero.

THE DISCIPLES MEET THE RISEN LORD

Matt. 28:16–20

I T IS SIGNIFICANT that this final disciple character-shaping incident is also the last event in Matthew's narrative. As the expanded chart depicts, there are a number of sections in the last two chapters of the narrative in which Jesus is not "on scene." Nevertheless, Jesus twice directs teaching to the disciples. It is significant for the T-CR, given their negative portrayal, that the disciples themselves are not "on scene" until near the end of the story. Two of the "responses" noted on the chart are not in reply to actions and words of Jesus but denote (1) the action of the women "who had followed Jesus from Galilee" (27:55), and (2) the burial of Jesus by Joseph of Arimathea, depicted as "a disciple of Jesus" (27:57). In the character-shaping response, the eleven disciples react to Jesus' appearance. The response occurs before the narrator reports Jesus' final statement and commands.

Details of Event

The narrative ends with the disciples and Jesus coming together again after a lengthy separation. The narrator describes the disciples' action and attitude briefly. Jesus' final statement, addressed to the disciples only, is about his status and their responsibility.

> [16]Now the eleven disciples went to Galilee, to the mountain to which Jesus had directed them. [17]And when they saw him they worshipped him; but they doubted. [18]And Jesus came and said to them, "All authority in heaven and on earth has been given to me. [19]Go therefore and make disciples of all nations, baptizing them in the name of the Father and of the Son and of the Holy Spirit, [20]teaching them to observe all that I have commanded you; and lo, I am with you always, to the close of the age."

Matthew's narrative reaches its climax in Galilee, after the tense situations in Jerusalem. The disciples return to the area where their call took place (10:1) and where most of Jesus' teaching occurred. The mountain in Galilee where this scene occurs is not identified. It could be the mountain of Jesus' first teaching (chapters 5–7) or the mountain of the transfiguration (17:2–6). The narrator has also informed the T-CR that Jesus twice had retreated to a mountain, once by himself (14:23) and once followed by the crowd (15:29). Thus, although the word "mountain" has been used many times, the T-CR is given no information about exactly where this concluding event occurs. In any case, the disciples are back in Galilee, where most of Jesus' career took place, and a significant distance from Jerusalem, the location of his death and resurrection.

Although the disciples are not told in the narrative, the T-CR is aware that they *do* know of Jesus' resurrection. The reason for going to Galilee is that Jesus "directed" them ("I will go before you to Galilee," 26:32); their action is the kind of response that Jesus expected. Thus the T-CR is informed that they have obeyed Jesus. The narrator also reports that they worshipped him when "they saw him" (28:17), although they doubted. Given the definition of character-shaping incident used in this study, there is no *direct* disciple response within the incident. But as the concluding incident in the narrative, it gives the T-CR disciple-related material and completes their portrayal in this narrative world. Specific gaps to which the T-CR is exposed may be "filled" by the context. Jesus is quoted as teaching in his final appearance, but there is no description of the way he looked to the disciples or of any actions that he performed.

Because the disciples fled when Jesus was arrested and were not present at his crucifixion, this incident, coming after the resurrection, introduces the T-CR to a change in their portrait. They again are portrayed as followers and listeners when the narrator reports that they meet with the risen Jesus in Galilee, in accordance with his earlier command.

The implication that they go to Galilee is positive, but they are also described with the words: "They worshipped him, but they doubted" (28:17). The narrator has used the word "worship" most often to describe how certain characters respond to Jesus, who only used the word twice himself. He spoke of worshipping "the Lord your God" (4:10) when responding to the devil's request for worship, and also used the word in a story about a servant responding to his king (18:26). The word appeared three times in the framework story about the Magi: to indicate why the Magi followed the star (2:2); by Herod who claimed he would also like to worship the child the Magi sought (2:8); and by the narrator to describe the Magis' response when they found "the child"

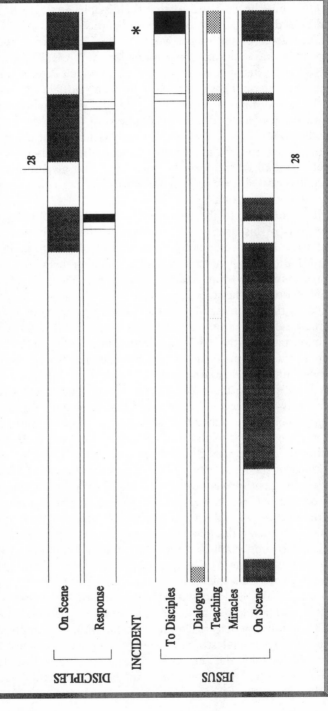

Disciple Character-Shaping Analysis #11: Matthew 28:16–20
Expanded Section: Matthew 27:11–28:20

(2:11). Thus the T-CR learns that the disciples in 28:17 have a positive understanding of Jesus' authority and status.

The narrator's use of the word "doubt" in direct relation to "worship" does have specific implications for the T-CR. The word appeared only in character-shaping incident four, in which Peter is unable to continue walking on the water because he is "afraid." He is then questioned by Jesus: "O man of little faith, why did you doubt?" (14:31). The conjunction of Peter's fear and doubt with the word "faith" becomes significant for the T-CR when the word "doubt" appears again in 28:17, at the conclusion of the narrative, to describe the disciples immediately after they had worshipped the risen Lord. But given other paradoxical combinations of attributes in the narrative, the combination of terms here is not surprising.

Jesus' teaching to the disciples (28:18–20) begins by stating the implications of his death and resurrection, that is, that he has received authority. The teaching is followed by a command to make disciples of all the nations through baptism and by teaching them "to observe all that I have commanded you" (28:19). Thus their teaching would be based on large sections of the story encompassing Jesus' speeches. After this command to the disciples, Matthew's story concludes with Jesus' reference to the future: He promises to be with them until the end of the age.

Important for the T-CR's understanding of the disciples, the resurrected Jesus informs them, not about his experience of death, but about the meaning of his resurrection: "All authority in heaven and on earth has been given to me" (28:18). The word "authority" had been used previously to refer to Jesus' teaching and healing. Authority was the main issue for the centurion, whom Jesus said had faith (8:9); authority is given to the disciples (though they did not use it, 10:1); and Jesus' authority is questioned by opponents (21:23). Thus Jesus expresses the meaning of the resurrection for this narrative world as his reception of all authority in heaven and earth. He already had authority to teach, to cast out demons, to heal, and to forgive sins. The implication is that he now has *more* authority, and thus it is appropriate to command the disciples to make disciples of all nations.

It is also important that the T-CR, who already has a complex portrait of the disciples, is now informed, at the conclusion of the narrative that the word "disciple" can be used more positively. Its meaning does not depend on the followers having complied with all of Jesus' expectations. Being told to "make disciples of all the nations" means, for the T-CR, guiding people to be like the disciples. The implication is that future followers of Jesus will receive the same commands, but will apparently resemble the current disciples as people of little faith, having doubt and fear, but people who nonetheless "worship" the risen Jesus as the son of the Father.

Jesus' emphasis on baptism is also relatively new for the T-CR. The word was connected with the work of John the Baptist and with Jesus' baptism but has not appeared in the narrative world since the framework. It was not mentioned in any of Jesus' stated expectations for the disciples prior to this conclusion. Even more unusual for the T-CR is the phrase explaining the importance of baptism: "Baptize them in the name of the Father, Son, and Holy Spirit." Father and son were important figures throughout the narrative world, but the Holy Spirit was mentioned in only three other situations. The T-CR was initially informed of the Holy Spirit as the source of the birth of Jesus, and as a term used by the narrator and an angel of the Lord (1:18, 20). Also, John the Baptist says that his successor will baptize with the Holy Spirit and fire (3:11).

The most important context for the T-CR for gaining information about the Holy Spirit occurs in chapter 12, in which Jesus' dialogue with the Pharisees and opponents first becomes prominent. "Spirit" occurs in a quote from Isaiah (12:18); when Jesus refers to the source of his power to cast out demons (12:28); when Jesus speaks about unforgivable blasphemy against the Spirit (12:31), adding that whoever speaks against the Holy Spirit will not be forgiven (12:32); and finally when Jesus tells the story of a person lacking a clean spirit (12:43–45). Although an "unclean spirit" is cast out, it brings seven other unclean spirits who find no other spirit in the person previously "cleansed."

Thus the T-CR has received positive information about the Holy Spirit as a force closely connected to the Father. For the T-CR the combination of Father, Son and Holy Spirit at the conclusion of the narrative brings together three closely related forces. The disciples are commanded to perform actions they have not been asked to do previously, and to recognize that the action depends, not on their status, but on the authority of Jesus, the Father, and the Holy Spirit.

As a result, Jesus' final speech implies clearly that he accepts the disciples and recognizes their potential, not merely by speaking to them about his own new status, but by commanding them to do what they have not previously done: baptize and teach. But, the most important factor indicating that he accepts them, despite their limitations, is that he uses the verb "to disciple" when describing what they are expected to do. The T-CR thus gets every indication that the disciples' limitations should not paralyze them. Jesus want them to act on his behalf and states that he will accompany them in the days to come, before the end of the age.

Context

The context for incident eleven, which describes the circumstances preceding the conclusion of the story, details the activities of Jesus' opponents to crucify him, the specifics of the crucifixion, its effect on certain individuals, and Jesus' burial and resurrection.

The previous disciple character-shaping incident included the report of Judas's repentance, his rejection by the chief priests, and his suicide. It ended with a fulfillment quotation indicating that his action and death were not beyond the control of the Father. After Judas's response when Jesus is delivered to Pilate (27:2), the narrator describes the confrontation between Jesus and Pilate (27:11–14). The narrator emphasizes both Jesus' silence and his simple answers. The incident ends with the narrator's statement that Pilate "wondered greatly" (27:14) because of Jesus' unwillingness to speak in defense of the accusations against him.

The T-CR's understanding of the disciples is influenced by a variety of details in this portion of the narrative. To explain the governor Pilate's response, the narrator supplies background information about a traditional release of a prisoner during this feast (27:15). Pilate's offer to release Jesus, rather than Barabbas, a "notorious prisoner" (27:16), is based on his understanding that the Jewish authorities had delivered Jesus out of "envy" (27:18). Thus the T-CR is informed that Pilate disagrees with the Sanhedrin. To help explain Pilate's reluctance to comply with the Jewish authorities, the narrator reports that Pilate's wife had advised him to "have nothing to do with that righteous man" (27:19) because of her dream. The word "dream" had been used previously to inform the T-CR about how God, the Father, influenced Joseph at the time of Mary's pregnancy. The statement by Pilate's wife provides another reason for questioning the Sanhedrin's purpose in demanding Jesus' death. Thus the narrator has given the T-CR a number of reasons for Pilate's reluctance to accept the Sanhedrin's judgment against Jesus.

The negative portrayal of the chief priests and elders continues with the next report that they have persuaded the crowd to ask for Barabbas, not Jesus (27:20). Pilate finally is reported to agree with Jesus' opponents to avoid a riot (27:24). When he washes his hands to illustrate his disagreement, the response of the people, "His blood be upon us and on our children" (27:25), shows the T-CR that these "people" accept responsibility for the condemnation of Jesus.

The crucifixion is then reported in detail (27:27–54). The soldiers mock Jesus as King of the Jews (27:27–31). Simon of Cyrene carries the cross as the procession moves to Golgotha, and Jesus is offered wine mixed with gall (27:32–34). Various forms of antagonism are reported: the placement of the sign describing Jesus as King of the Jews (27:37), the derision of people passing by (27:39–40), the continued mocking of chief priests and elders (27:41–43), and the taunts of the two crucified robbers (27:44). Thus, the crucifixion story focuses on the reactions of people rather than the suffering of Jesus. Since the disciples are not mentioned, it is clear to the T-CR that they have indeed run away and abandoned him.

Jesus' death is reported as the conclusion to rejection by various groups of Jewish people (27:45–50). After reporting a darkness over the land, the narrator quotes Jesus' question, "My God, My God, why have you forsaken me?" The question becomes the basis for the final mockery. The narrator reports that bystanders, who think Jesus beseeches Elijah, attempt to give him liquid in order to prolong his life, to see if indeed Elijah will rescue him. The T-CR has learned, however, that Elijah has come in the form of John the Baptist and has been killed by Herod in Galilee. Herod had ordered the murder to keep peace and balance in his territory and among his supporters; thus Herod was acting like Pilate. Immediately after the final mockery, the narrator reports that "Jesus cried again with a loud voice and yielded up his spirit" (27:50).

Jesus' death results in three distinct events: the tearing of the curtain in the temple (27:51); the shaking of the earth and the awakening of many saints, who roam after Jesus is raised (27:51–53); and the response of the centurion, who, having witnessed the earthquake, declares that Jesus is indeed the Son of God (27:54). All of these events fit clearly in the world of this narrative where God, the Father, is active. Although they do not fulfill specific predictions, the events correspond with the world presented to the T-CR. Most significant for the T-CR is that the disciples are not present; they are "off scene" and therefore do not witness the events reported after the death of Jesus. The negative portrayal of the eleven followers does not change, since they are no longer part of the story.

On the other hand "many women" *are* reported as witnesses (27:55). The narrator states that they were "looking on from afar" and that they had followed Jesus from Galilee (27:55). Neither these women, nor their action as followers, had been mentioned previously in this narrative world. Since they reportedly followed Jesus to witness his death, they are presented to the T-CR, by comparison to the absent disciples, as the right kind of disciple, that is, as more faithful. The narrator lists the names of three of the women, "Mary Magdalene, and Mary the mother of James and Joseph, and the mother of the sons of Zebedee" (27:56), to emphasize their presence. The absence of the eleven disciples is thereby reemphasized for the T-CR.

The next report, about Joseph of Arimathea (27:57–60), called "a disciple of Jesus" also helps emphasize the absence of the eleven. Joseph gets permission to take Jesus' body, and he buries Jesus in a "new" tomb. Since this is the only time that Joseph is mentioned, it is important that the narrator calls him a disciple, thereby informing the T-CR that the term "disciple" is not limited to the chosen twelve. Joseph is similar to the women who stay close to Jesus and witness his crucifixion and death. Also, two of the women, reported to witness Jesus' death, witness the burial (27:61).

This section of the story continues to inform the T-CR about the disciples by reporting the request by the chief priests and Pharisees to set up a guard at the tomb (27:62–66). The guard is to prevent the disciples from stealing Jesus' body and claiming a resurrection. Pilate remains unwilling to be directly involved, telling the Jewish authorities to take care of this concern on their own. Thus, with their request, Jesus' opponents act consistently with their earlier characterization and make explicit their animosity toward the disciples.

The resurrection account (28:1–10) reports the continuing activity of two of the women, Mary Magdalene and the other Mary, who witness a second earthquake which occurs because of the appearance of an angel opening the tomb. After the narrator reports the strange reaction of the guards, the angel commands the women to verify that the tomb is empty. They are told to give the disciples the message to meet Jesus in Galilee, informing the T-CR that the disciples remain a major concern for Jesus, despite their withdrawal. The narrator describes the women as fearful, but joyful, and then reports that they meet the risen Jesus. When the narrator reports that they "took hold of his feet" and worshipped him, the T-CR is informed of Jesus' physical reality and their understanding of his authority.

Jesus' words, the first words of the risen Lord, are also significant for the T-CR: "Do not be afraid" (28:10). The words reflect an attitude important earlier in the narrative and that is distinct from faith. Jesus repeats the angel's command to send the disciples to Galilee (28:7), itself a repetition of Jesus' promise in 26:32. The disciples, however, are now referred to as "my brethren."

This is the second time Jesus has used the term "brethren" for the disciples. When he responded to an attempt by his mother and brothers to speak to him, he asked, "Who are my mother and brothers?" (12:48). Jesus said the disciples are his mother and brethren because the term describes anyone who "does the will of my Father in heaven." He also called both the crowd and the disciples "brethren" when contrasting them to the hypocrites. He told them not to call themselves "rabbi," because they have one teacher and "are all brethren" (23:8). Thus the T-CR is informed that, although the disciples have been portrayed negatively, the risen Jesus refers to them as "brethren," indicating his positive attitude toward them though they do not meet his expectations. The T-CR sees Jesus' positive expression toward the disciples, despite their inability to act as he expects.

Immediate Context

The incident preceding the final character-shaping incident and the conclusion of the story reports that the guards receive bribes from the chief priests and elders to say that the disciples are responsible for Jesus' reported resurrection (28:11–15). After describing the incident, the narrator states that "this story has been spread among the Jews to this day" (28:15). The story not only reinforces the description of the resurrection, but also verifies the lack of involvement from the disciples. The narrator emphasizes the opponents' explicit action against the disciples' reputation and perhaps explains why "to this day" some consider the disciples inadequate followers. The event also prepares the T-CR for the final scene, which reaffirms the disciples as "positive" followers, accepted by Jesus and distinct from the opponents.

Summary

After being informed of the repentance and suicide of Judas, the T-CR can see that the opponents will likely complete their assault of Jesus. Judas could not reverse his action and therefore committed suicide. Although the eleven other disciples had not betrayed Jesus, they had fled, and Peter had been unwilling even to admit his status as a follower/disciple. Without any attempt from disciples to defend Jesus, the action of Pilate helps emphasize the negative character of the opponents for the T-CR. Pilate disagrees with the Jewish authorities' indictment of Jesus, but is unwilling to stand against them because of the support they have from the crowd. For the T-CR Pilate is not portrayed as an opponent.

The crucifixion itself is reported to take place without the support or presence of the eleven disciples. But three women and Joseph of Arimathea are depicted as followers. That certain groups mock Jesus is made clear to the T-CR. In addition, that a centurion calls Jesus the "Son of God" in response to an earthquake at the time of death, puts negative emphasis on the T-CR's image of the disciples.

Although the disciples are not present in this section of the narrative, the T-CR receives information that adds to the complexity of their character as a group. They become the object of discussion when the angel and Jesus both ask for the disciples to go to Galilee. Having Jesus refer to them as "my brethren" adds positive weight to the T-CR's image of followers who have not followed. As followers they have fled. Despite their withdrawal, Jesus has not rejected them, because they apparently have not ceased being followers/disciples.

Thus in the conclusion of the narrative the T-CR gains a positive view of the disciples, though when described as "worshipping" Jesus they are

also described as "doubting." They had been often portrayed as followers of "little faith." This characteristic has continued. However, Jesus'
final command indicates that he accepts their limited capability — they
are to become "disciple-makers," both by baptizing and teaching "all
nations." Jesus, the one with full authority, gives them a task more
elaborate than previous expectations.

CONCLUSION

A NARRATIVE ANALYSIS of the disciples in Matthew's gospel should emphasize how the T-CR, the text-connoted reader, has been informed about the disciples. In order to understand the world of this narrative and to comprehend the portrayal of the disciples, it is necessary to look carefully at the flow of the incidents and at the disciples' actions and words. The analysis will help one comprehend how the material has influenced the hypothetical reader, the T-CR. As a conclusion to this narrative analysis, it is therefore appropriate to summarize the characterization of the disciples.

The keys to understanding how the disciples are portrayed are the specifics of this narrative world. One must focus on how the narrator reports the disciples' thoughts and their reactions to events and/or statements from other characters. The disciples are not the main characters in the narrative. Jesus, the most important character, is clearly portrayed as the son of the Father and is, in part, portrayed by stating his expectations of the disciples, both by teaching them and by responding to their words and actions.

Because Matthew's gospel is a relatively long narrative, one must begin with the first presentation of the disciples and then examine any incident in which their peculiarities and dispositions are revealed. One can then compile an accurate portrait of the disciples as given to the T-CR. The eleven disciple *character-shaping incidents* must be analyzed in their narrative order.

In incident one, Jesus invites four men to become "fishers of people" by "following" him. The response indicates their willingness to change their life. The reason they leave their jobs as fishermen and take a new role as followers of Jesus, as well as their specific understanding of Jesus' command and statement, is not described for the T-CR.

In incident two, after the disciples learn about Jesus' expectations, they awaken him when they are afraid of drowning in the sea. They make clear that they do not understand exactly who he is; Jesus calls them "men of little faith." Thus they are portrayed as limited followers.

In incident three, after Jesus teaches the disciples using parables, they appear to be intelligent followers who claim to understand Jesus' metaphorical teaching. In addition, Jesus' response to their answer is apparently positive and challenging thereby indicating to the T-CR Jesus' belief that they have made progress as his followers.

In incident four, Peter appears to have a positive understanding of Jesus, although a restricted one, when he cannot walk on the sea for more than a few steps. However, after Jesus and Peter enter the boat, the narrator reports that Peter and the other disciples worship Jesus and call him the Son of God. The T-CR receives both a negative and positive portrait. The disciples appear to be complex characters.

In incident five, the T-CR sees another involved presentation of the disciples' character when Jesus praises Peter for recognizing the Father's influence by understanding Jesus as the Father's son. After he rebukes Jesus for predicting his (Jesus') death and resurrection, Peter is criticized as evil. Peter and the disciples become more complex characters as detail is added, especially from promising and critical responses to their behavior.

In incident six, Peter, James, and John see a transfigured Jesus, and Peter responds positively to this vision. Though Peter is interrupted by the voice from heaven, and thereby seems criticized, the result is positive for the T-CR's assessment when the narrator reports that the three disciples do indeed listen to Jesus and understand him.

In incident seven, the portrait becomes more negative. In response to Jesus' teaching about human limitations to reaching the kingdom of heaven, the disciples raise questions about their status. Despite Jesus' emphasis on his death, they continue to show that their faith does not meet Jesus' expectations.

In incident eight, Judas, one of the twelve disciples, becomes a betrayer by cooperating with Jesus' opponents, the chief priests. Thus the T-CR sees that one of the chosen followers has become an opponent of Jesus.

In incident nine, the negative portrait continues. Peter, James, and John fall asleep; they cannot stay alert as Jesus required. Then Judas acts as the betrayer by having Jesus arrested. Peter, who claims to be a true follower, follows Jesus at a distance, but will not admit that he is one of Jesus' followers. So the T-CR is now given more information about why Jesus described the disciples as men of little faith.

In incident ten, the suicide of Judas functions as self-criticism when he finds out that Jesus has been condemned. He is portrayed as a repentant betrayer, but his original intention in betraying Jesus is still not reported. To the T-CR, Judas, as a disciple, appears to be a complete failure.

In incident eleven, the conclusion of the narrative, there is an unusual portrayal containing both positive and negative elements. The eleven disciples go to Galilee, as Jesus had directed, and, upon seeing the risen Lord, they worship and doubt. They are portrayed as followers — men of little faith, but not *without* faith. When Jesus addresses them positively it is a distinct change for the T-CR. Despite their limited capabilities, Jesus accepts them as followers and asks them to make disciples of all nations. To be a disciple is to be baptized by the Father, Son and Holy Spirit, and also to know and understand all that Jesus taught his disciples before his death and resurrection.

Given this information about the narrative flow and development informing the T-CR, it is now possible to state what the text-connoted *author* (T-CA) says about the disciples. The T-CA, like the T-CR, is a hypothetical construct based on the narrative world. Once we know how the T-CR has been informed throughout the story, we can now put it all together and seek to understand the primary emphasis of the T-CA. What is the T-CA's overall understanding of the disciples?

The most important feature of this narrative world is that, at the beginning, the disciples are invited to become "fishers of people" by following Jesus. Then, at the conclusion of the narrative, they are told to make disciples of all nations. Jesus, the main character, who at the conclusion is described as having full authority, gives the eleven disciples the meaning of his metaphorical statement that they are to become fishers of people: "Go therefore and make disciples of all nations, baptizing them in the name of the Father and of the Son and of the Holy Spirit, teaching them to observe all that I have commanded you; and lo, I am with you always, to the close of the age" (28:19–20). Despite the disciples' positive and negative characteristics in the flow of the story, they have been followers in enough ways to be asked to be "disciple-makers." The risen Jesus has also said that they are his brethren! So a disciple, according to the T-CA, is not an ideal individual who meets Jesus' expectations, but one who recognizes Jesus and who will follow him, in a limited fashion, under most conditions.

The word "disciple" was used generally at first, then was used to refer to the named twelve, then was used much later to refer to followers not among the twelve, and finally was used as a verb when the risen Jesus gave the eleven disciples their final command. Given this flow and development, the T-CA portrays the followers of Jesus, after his resurrection, as those who try to meet Jesus' expectations, but who probably will not be able to: They worship but they doubt. The T-CA does not expect any disciple to fulfill Jesus' expectations; a follower of Jesus may be fully aware of what Jesus wants but will not be able to meet this ideal. Although they may not meet Jesus' requirements, the disciples are still acceptable as "fishers of people" when they worship — even doubt — Jesus as the son of the Father, when they baptize in the name of the Father, Son, and Holy Spirit, and when they recognize the importance of Jesus' teachings and encourage others to become disciples.

Index to the Gospel of Matthew